# THOSE THREE DAYS

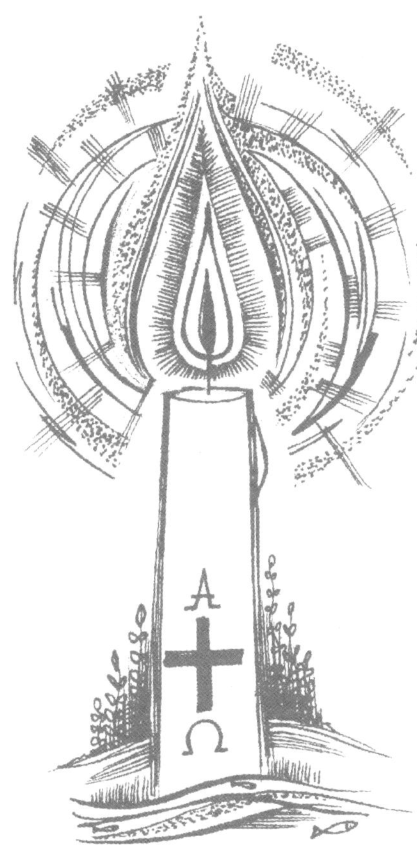


## A RESOURCE FOR THE CELEBRATION OF THE EASTER TRIDUUM

COMPILED BY
JOHN McCANN AND PAT O'DONOGHUE

VERITAS

*First published 2002 by*
Veritas Publications
7/8 Lower Abbey Street
Dublin 1
Ireland

Email publications@veritas.ie
Website www.veritas.ie

ISBN 1 85390 655 7



A catalogue record for this book is available from the British Library.



Designed by Colette Dower
Printed in the Republic of Ireland by Betaprint Ltd, Dublin

*Veritas books are printed on paper made from the wood pulp of managed forests. For every tree felled, at least one tree is planted, thereby renewing natural resources.*

# CONTENTS

# THOSE THREE DAYS - INTRODUCTION

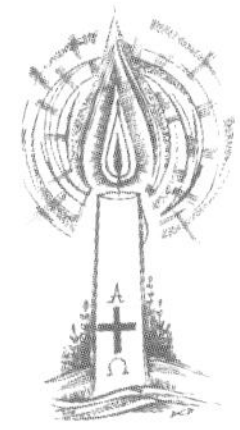

PAT O'DONOGHUE

There is something to be learnt from the fact that many churches are thronged for the Celebration of the Lord's Passion, in some form or other, on Good Friday. The drama of the Way of the Cross captured in image and word and the act of veneration seem to touch people who may not form part of the weekly celebration of the Eucharist.

Those who may not understand the meaning of the word 'Mandatum' may, however, live their lives in that model of service without making an explicit connection with this distinctive ritual of the Holy Thursday liturgy.

Vigil is experienced by people who queue up all night for those precious concert tickets, though they probably do not make the connection with the Easter Vigil and what it could mean. Even the word 'triduum' is not in the vocabulary of many who would, however, understand the idea of a 'three-day event'.

The presentation and celebration of 'Those Three Days' needs to be done in such a way that it captures the attention of those who are hungering for spiritual nourishment and yet do not find their way to participate in the celebration of the most important days in the Church's calendar.

To return to the Good Friday experience, it seems that the act of veneration is the high point. Participation and an identification with the reality of life may be the key factors here. The question then is how to translate this observation, if true, to the other liturgies of the triduum.

*Those Three Days* is a practical collection of material for use in the preparation and celebration of the liturgies on the days of the triduum. The principal liturgies are explored and helpful ideas shared. There are resources for music ministers, sacristans and celebrants. This collection also contains resources that would be useful for groups preparing at a spiritual level for the celebration of the Easter Triduum.

New material includes two liturgies for celebrations around the cross and a Way of the Cross. The Old Testament readings of the vigil are the subject of another prayerful and reflective resource for all involved in the celebration of this liturgy. There are ideas for a Mass with Children on Holy Thursday and for the service of prayer that evening.

Our hope is that you will find it helpful, whether as a celebrant, a minister or a participant in the liturgies of these grace-filled days. Farm out the preparatory tasks to as many groups as possible depending on your human resources. Use the material as a source of spiritual enrichment on your Lenten journey so that the different dynamics of the various liturgies will come through.

# THINKING ABOUT THE TRIDUUM AS A WHOLE

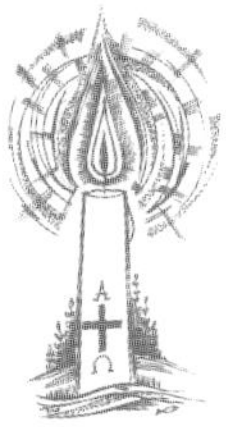

JOHN MCCANN

Before one gets into the 'nuts and bolts' of each celebration within the Easter Triduum, it is good now and then to stand back from it all and look at the triduum as a whole. It's good to ask questions: Which are the most important celebrations of the triduum? What are the priorities? What is the overall shape of the triduum?

**The Importance of the Triduum**

In the reform of the liturgy after Vatican II, the Easter Triduum is seen as the 'most solemn of all feasts' and the 'summit of the liturgical year'. It deserves the very best that we can give it. People will expect celebrations that are truly uplifting and profound. Generally they are quite happy to take time at things in these holy days. People don't want authentic celebration to be sacrificed on the altar of 'practicality'. Given the importance of these celebrations, parish liturgy groups might well begin to prepare for them even at the beginning of Lent, or earlier.

**The Unity of the Triduum**

The earliest annual paschal celebrations among Christians were almost certainly on a single day, coinciding with the date of the Jewish Passover. Fairly soon, this feast was probably preceded by two days of fasting. By the time of St Augustine, the meaning of the three days was articulated as referring to three distinct moments within the Christian Passover: Christ crucified, buried and risen. With the advent of pilgrimages to the Holy Land, the desire to relive *in situ* each moment of the final events leading up to the death of Christ led to a further emphasis on each distinct event. The traditional Stations of the Cross are a classic example of this. This brief historical sketch shows two values at work within the triduum: first, the (earlier) unity of the celebration, and second, the (later) diversity of moments. Both approaches are legitimate and are ideally held in tension. If we err on any side today, it is probably in the direction of splitting up the celebration too much into its distinct moments. And yet there are signs of that fundamental unity everywhere in the liturgical rites: on Good Friday we hear the passion according to John, which interprets the passion very much in the light of the Resurrection as a triumphant moment; on Good Friday, too, our reception of the Eucharist might alert us to the fact that we celebrate the death of one who is now risen and with us; the paschal candle is ritually marked by the wounds of Christ – it is, in a sense, 'bloodstained'; the Easter Vigil is no easy triumph but, like the appearances of the risen Jesus in the upper room, shows the scars of death.

**The Days of the Triduum are Friday, Saturday, Sunday**

The interpretation of the triduum as referring to Christ crucified, buried and risen corresponds to the three days: Friday, Saturday and Sunday. We may have a tendency to see the triduum as 'Thursday to Saturday'. This is probably a remnant of the days when all the celebrations were anticipated by many hours, with the Easter Vigil happening on Saturday morning, and corresponding celebrations on Thursday and Friday mornings. When the timing of the days gets mixed up, the practical outcome is that Holy Saturday as a celebration of Christ buried disappears.

There is no 'waiting by the tomb'. To remedy this, we include in this resource book some material for use on Holy Saturday morning.

**The Vigil is the High Point of the Triduum**

The vigil is the last of the major celebrations of the triduum (the celebrations do, however, continue into the rest of Sunday, with other celebrations of the Eucharist and the Liturgy of the Hours). Being the last celebration, it is in danger of getting the least preparation, when energies are beginning to run out. It is important then to get the priorities right from the beginning: in the advanced planning, it is the vigil that needs the greatest amount of work and resources.

**The Sacramental Dimension of the Triduum is All-Important**

The celebrations of the triduum are not just a mental recalling of past events. It's not in the last analysis an attempt to recreate scenes that were lived almost two thousand years ago. It is above all an action in which we ourselves are marked by the dying and rising of Jesus. The purpose of the triduum is that the pattern of his paschal mystery is imprinted onto our lives. Through our acceptance in faith of God's word and our participation in the sacraments, we too die and rise with Christ, even now. This explains the emphasis on Baptism within the Easter Vigil. New candidates are plunged into the death and resurrection of Christ at the font. Those of us who are already baptised renew our commitment to live fully this journey of life-through-death, and we are even sprinkled with baptismal waters as a tangible reminder. The Vigil Eucharist crowns our participation in the death and resurrection of Jesus: when we participate in his body and blood given for humanity, we too pledge to give ourselves and to be part of his sacrificial gift.

**Let's Not Forget the Triduum Fast**

From the earliest times fasting was part of the triduum. Although Lent, with its various liturgical and ascetic practices, finishes on Holy Thursday, the solemn fast of the triduum then begins. The Vatican II *Constitution on the Liturgy* put it this way: 'The Paschal fast must be kept sacred. It should be celebrated everywhere on Good Friday, and where possible should be prolonged throughout Holy Saturday so that the faithful may attain the joys of the Sunday of the resurrection with uplifted and responsive minds' (110). For those who are working hard to prepare the liturgies, some wise moderation in fasting suggests itself; but one imagines that by and large we are more likely to err in the opposite direction and forget the fast altogether.

**The Celebrations Continue for Fifty Days**

The earliest Christian references to 'Pentecost' use it to refer not so much to the fiftieth day (now Pentecost Sunday) as to the whole fifty days of Easter. They are, in a sense, one big long Easter Sunday. This is reflected, for example, in the name given to the Sundays after Easter Sunday: no longer are they called 'Sundays after Easter', but 'Sundays of Easter'. The readings throughout this season from the Acts of the Apostles and the Gospel according to John reflect brightly the light of the Resurrection. Some thought might be given to finding various ways of keeping the sense of festivity alive:

- The paschal candle is kept lighting at all liturgies. After Pentecost Sunday it is removed to the baptistry and only appears in the sanctuary thereafter for funerals.
- Look at how the church building is decorated.
- Replace the penitential rite with the blessing and sprinkling of water on Sundays.
- Consider singing the *Gloria* more often during this season.
- Be more lavish in your use of traditional liturgical signs: candles, incense, music, etc.
- This is an ideal time for communion under both kinds.
- Plan an 'Easter Garden', either inside the church (but away from the altar) or outside.

# HOLY THURSDAY
# EVENING MASS OF THE LORD'S SUPPER

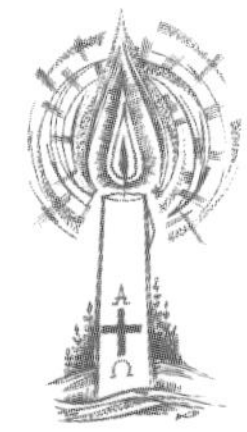

John McCann

**What are We Celebrating Tonight?**

While every Mass recalls in some way the Last Supper, this evening's Mass remembers the Last Supper in a particular way: this was the moment when Jesus gave us the gift of the Eucharist and the priesthood; he also gave us the teaching and example of humble love. As such, this celebration touches a precious moment in the life of Jesus that is profound, mysterious and yet intimate. We will, therefore, want to celebrate this liturgy with particular love, gratitude and care. Tonight's celebration must, nonetheless, be seen within a larger context. It is part of a triduum whose climax is the Easter Vigil. The Vigil Eucharist is, in a sense, the Eucharist of the triduum, and should be experienced as such. The Vigil Eucharist should be marked by even greater solemnity and should be even more lavish in its celebration. To put it rather mundanely: we need to keep something in reserve for the Easter Vigil. It is no harm to remember, too, that Good Friday is, strictly speaking, the first day of the triduum. Holy Thursday evening is the threshold of Good Friday, just as the Easter Vigil is the crossover into Easter Sunday, thc moment of 'passing' from fast to feast, from death to glory. The giving of Christ's body, handed over for us, and his blood, poured out for us, speak of his generosity unto death. The Last Supper and the Cross belong together.

**The Introductory Rite**

As people gather, a short music practice will help them to participate more fully. Some brief comments about the celebration may be helpful, to give people a 'map' of what will happen. Let's not, however, start trying to explain everything. The symbols of the triduum are eloquent and speak to us on many levels – too much explanation will rob them of their power. If well done, the symbolic actions of these days will have their effect, even if they are not fully understood. There is always more to a symbol than what is immediately available to our intellectual grasp. As always, comments, notices or music practices are best conducted from a place other than the ambo, which is sacred to the Word of God.

The entrance procession moves from the sacristy through the church (going outside if necessary). The procession might be ordered as follows:

- Thurible and incense bearers
- Cross bearer
- Two candle bearers
- Other ministers, as needed
- The Book of Gospels, carried by a reader
- Concelebrants
- The presiding priest

If the parish has an aumbry (a special receptacle for the Holy Oils), the oils blessed at the Mass of Chrism could also be carried in procession and placed therein. The oil bearers could walk in the procession after the candle bearers.

The presider kisses and incenses the altar in the usual way. The solemnity of the occasion also suggests the use of incense at other moments of the liturgy: the Gospel, the Preparation of the Gifts and the Procession to the Place of Repose.

Hopefully the *Gloria* will be sung this evening, and thus it might be preferable to recite the penitential rite. This part of the Mass is, after all, only introductory. Version C (vi) of the penitential rite seems particularly suitable, as it includes the words, 'Lord Jesus, you feed us with your body and blood'.

The singing of the *Gloria* is traditionally accompanied by the ringing of bells and vigorous instrumental playing. The use of musical instruments thereafter is discreet. If there are young altar servers, bells are best removed from their orbit, lest they sound again before the Easter Vigil!

**The Liturgy of the Word**

This evening's readings present quite a challenge to the ministers of the word. The first reading in particular may come across as a rather irrelevant account of obsolete ritual prescriptions, and yet when properly understood it adds new depth to our understanding of the Eucharist. The Passover meal, described in this reading, is a solemn act of remembrance. It recalls liberation from slavery, a new beginning, a journey into new life, with the blood of the Passover Lamb serving as a sign of God's protection. The story of the liberation from the slavery of Egypt was to be a sign to each successive generation of the God who saves. Each Passover meal was a symbolic entering into the primordial event of the Exodus, a new experience of the saving presence of God and, as such, a basis for future hopes. The meal was in memory of the Exodus. The words of Jesus 'Do this as a memorial of me', recounted in the second reading, take on new force when we realise that the Last Supper took place within a Passover context. The saving event that we now enter into is Jesus' own exodus to the Father. The liberation is from sin. Jesus himself is the Passover Lamb, given by God as a pledge of his continued presence and protection. The Gospel views the Last Supper from a different, though not unrelated, angle. Just where we might expect to find the narrative of the institution of the Eucharist, the Gospel according to John gives us the story of the washing of the feet. This eloquent action on the part of Jesus is clearly an example to be imitated, but it has also been said that, like the Eucharist, it is a prophetic sign of the servant death of Jesus. In this light we might say that, by washing the feet of his disciples, Jesus communicates through his actions what he communicates through his words in Mark 10:45:

> 'The Son of Man himself came not to be served but to serve, and to give his life as a ransom for many.'

It is interesting to note, too, that Peter, who had difficulty in accepting Jesus' predictions of his passion and death (Mk 8:32), is also the one who has difficulty in accepting the washing of feet. Tonight's readings might provoke us to ask: do we really accept the gift that Jesus gives us in these three days, let alone imitate it?

**A Gospel Procession**

A procession with the Book of Gospels seems appropriate to the solemnity of the celebration. It will be necessary for the Lectionary to be removed from the ambo before the procession, to make room for the Book of Gospels. The thurible and incense are brought to the presider at the chair, and he puts incense into the thurible. A deacon, concelebrant or, in their absence, the presider himself, goes to the altar and, taking the Book of Gospels, carries it solemnly around the sanctuary to the ambo, preceded by incense and candles. The book is incensed after the people acclaim the Gospel in the words 'Glory to you, Lord'. Those with candles and incense remain around the ambo until the Gospel reading is finished and then return to their places. In a small church it may be wise to keep the thurible in another room when not in use – consideration needs to be given to those who have respiratory problems and to singers.

**A Drama of Service: The Washing of the Feet**

The rite of foot-washing, which may take place after the homily, is the only instance of dramatic representation in the Roman liturgical books at present. Dramatic, quasi-theatrical representations of the events of salvation history appeared within the liturgy in the Middle Ages and were perhaps an attempt to overcome some of the deficiencies of the liturgies of that era. The approach of the renewal of the liturgy since Vatican II has been to address the deficiencies of the liturgy by modifying the liturgy itself rather than by inserting pieces of drama. Whenever there is a perceived need for drama this may in fact point to the need for a deeper renewal of sacramental life in the Church (as it did in the Middle Ages). Nonetheless, this small piece of liturgical theatre still remains with us. A few pointers may be helpful:

- Liturgical planners should resist the temptation to enact the foot-washing during the Gospel reading itself. The proclaimed text has its own way of communicating and carries many levels of meaning. The 'acting out' of the scene only presents some aspects of the text, and will obscure other layers of meaning if done simultaneously.

- It is a good idea to ensure that those whose feet are washed are broadly representative of the whole community.

- The presider takes off the chasuble for this rite. Not only is this practical, it also mirrors the actions of Jesus who 'removed his outer garment'.

- Chairs need to be provided for each of those whose feet are washed. In some churches a simple way to do this is to have each person sitting on a light chair in front of the front benches, from the beginning of Mass. When the time comes, each person simply lifts their own chair a few feet into the sanctuary and turns around to face the congregation. People who are elderly or disabled may need assistance. As a gesture of love, the washing of feet should be done with a certain generosity:

  Warm water (!), possibly perfumed with bath oils
  Beautiful jug and basin
  Plenty of towels (good hygiene!)

- The rite is accompanied by appropriate song. Music planners will get an idea of what is needed by looking at the texts proposed in the Missal. If there is congregational singing at this point, it seems a good idea to pick music that does not necessitate looking down at a participation sheet; otherwise the congregation will be looking at their sheets instead of at the rite itself.

**General Intercessions**

The general intercessions follow the washing of feet, or, if this does not take place, they follow the homily.

**Preparation of the Altar**

In preparation for the Eucharist, the corporal, chalice and water are brought to the altar from the side. The Missal is placed on the altar. This brief moment of preparation serves to articulate the movement from the Liturgy of the Word to the Liturgy of the Eucharist. It is preferable not to bring any vessels of bread or wine to the altar from the side. This will take away from the presentation of these gifts, which should come from among the congregation.

**A Real Act of Service: the Collection for the Poor**

The Missal suggests a procession of gifts for the poor at this point of the liturgy. This could be seen as a real act of service that puts into practice the ideals presented in the Gospel and the washing of the feet. There could be a collection in the usual way for a special cause, and the money could be brought forward. This could also be linked with other gifts collected in the preceding days or weeks, for example, Trócaire Lenten boxes, gifts of food or clothing for the needy. This approach also serves as a model for any non-eucharistic gifts that may be envisaged for Masses on other occasions. The gifts of bread and wine for the Eucharist are the last to be brought forward.

**The Eucharistic Prayer**

The Preface is that of the Holy Eucharist I.

The sung acclamations are particularly important. Consideration might be given to singing version (c), 'When we eat this bread…', as it is based on this evening's second reading. This version would make even more sense if communion is to be received under both kinds. While Eucharistic Prayer I may be too long for some congregations, it does have some special texts for use at this Mass, and so is worth considering. The texts in question are to be found in the Missal after the Prayer over the Gifts.

**The Communion Rite**

This Mass is a very suitable occasion for offering communion under both kinds to the congregation. For details, see the *General Instruction on the Roman Missal*, nn. 240-252.[1]

It is always timely to reflect critically on the kind of bread we use for the Eucharist, and no more so than this evening. The *General Instruction on the Roman Missal* tells us that the bread used by the priest should 'appear as actual food' and that it should be 'made in such a way that the priest can break it and distribute the parts to at least some of the faithful'.

This evening is also a particularly appropriate time for the Eucharist to be brought to those who are sick and housebound. The consecrated bread is brought to them directly from the altar.

**Transfer of the Blessed Sacrament**

Within the Catholic Church the Eucharist is reserved after the eucharistic celebration so that communion may be brought to those unable to attend Mass and so that further prayer may take place in the presence of the Blessed Sacrament. This devotion derives from the Mass and is directed towards further communion with Christ. These aspects of our eucharistic faith and practice are given special emphasis by the solemn reservation of the Eucharist which takes place this evening. This is reservation, not exposition, of the Blessed Sacrament.

1. It may also be helpful to consult diocesan guidelines or other pastoral resources. The Dublin Diocese, for example, published some helpful materials in *Recognising The Lord: Jubilee Resource Book 3* (Dublin Diocesan Jubilee Committee, 2000).

We also need to be careful that we do not impose other interpretations on this simple action. There was a time, for example, when the place of reservation was allegorised as a representation of the tomb of Christ, and indeed some of the tabernacles used (and still in use!) were designed to look like a casket. A more modern temptation is to try to turn the reservation of the Blessed Sacrament into a representation of the Garden of Olives. The focus here is on the Eucharist itself, with all the far-reaching consequences of this great gift.

After the Eucharist has been received, a ciborium containing the Blessed Sacrament is left on the altar, and Mass concludes with the Prayer after Communion. The priest incenses the Blessed Sacrament and then receives the humeral veil. The Blessed Sacrament is then carried in procession through the church to the place of reservation. The order of procession is as follows:

- Cross bearer
- Two or more candle bearers
- Other ministers
- One or two thurible bearers with burning incense
- The priest, carrying the Blessed Sacrament

During the procession a eucharistic song is sung.

When the procession arrives at the place of reservation, the ciborium is placed in the tabernacle, the door of which is left open. The priest incenses the Blessed Sacrament again. The door of the tabernacle is then closed. After a period of silent prayer, all rise, genuflect and return to the sacristy in silence.

There is no solemn blessing or dismissal to conclude this liturgy. This may be a relic of earlier centuries, when such elements were generally absent from the Mass, but it also points to the unity of these three days: the liturgy is not over, and will not conclude until the joyful *Alleluia, Alleluia* at the end of the Easter Vigil.

# HOLY THURSDAY - MASSES WITH CHILDREN

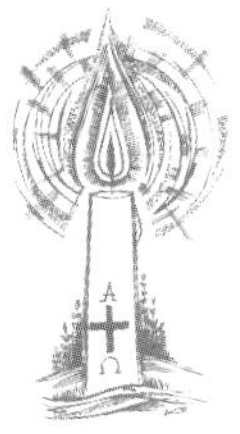

JOHN MCCANN

**A Special Mass for Children**

Many parishes have a special Mass for children some time before the adult Mass. This would be a suitable time to make some of the many adaptations that are permitted in the *Directory for Masses with Children,* for example:

- Not all of the elements in the Introductory Rite need be included.
- The Opening Prayer, Prayer over the Gifts and Prayer after Communion may be reworded to adapt to the children's level of comprehension.
- The number of readings may be reduced to two or even one (the Gospel may not, however, be omitted). This evening's first reading might well be dropped.
- The Responsorial Psalm may be replaced by a suitable psalm-type hymn.
- If only one reading is chosen, a hymn may be sung after the homily.
- The homily may be in the form of a dialogue. If necessary, someone other than the priest may address the children.
- The children may take different parts in the reading of a scriptural passage where the text suggests this kind of treatment. The Gospel of the washing of the feet would lend itself very well to this approach.
- Children may well be involved in the various processions: Entrance Procession, Gospel Procession, Procession of Gifts, Communion Procession. Children enjoy this kind of movement within the liturgy.
- Eucharistic Prayers for Children are possible.
- It is very important in children's Masses to say a few words before the final blessing, thus helping them to see the connection between liturgy and life.
- Artwork by the children can be appropriately used.

**An Adult Mass where Children are Present**

Many parishes have only one Mass on Holy Thursday evening and children are welcome to this. Some thought could be given to finding ways of involving them without compromising the solemn nature of the celebration.

As with the Mass at which few adults are present, children can be involved in the various processions:

- the Entrance Procession, carrying artwork, which is appropriately placed (not immediately in front of the altar or ambo);
- the Gospel Procession, carrying extra candles or flowers (the procession might move through the church building);
- the Procession of Gifts;
- children who are old enough to do so with safety might carry extra candles in the procession for the transfer of the Blessed Sacrament.

The *Directory for Masses with Children* makes provision for taking the children out from an adult Mass during the Liturgy of the Word. The children then have their own celebration of the Word. This could be done in the following way: After the Opening Prayer, the children are invited to line up in the main aisle of the church. Two servers with candles, accompanied by an adult, lead them in procession from the main body of the church into another room. In this room a table could be prepared in advance with a cloth and lighted candles, with the book of scriptures suitably displayed. When they all arrive in the room, the children sing a song in preparation for the Word. Two children pick up the candles on the table and hold them on either side of the book as the reading is proclaimed. After the reading, a qualified adult could dialogue briefly with the children about what they have heard. The children could then draw or colour in pictures of the Last Supper. It may be necessary to stop them before they are finished, in order to lead them back into the main assembly. In this case, they could take their pictures home and finish them whenever they like. Normally the children are not brought into the main celebrating area until the preparation of the gifts. If the washing of the feet is to take place, it might be better, however, to bring them back in time to see this happen.

Older children could help with the washing of the feet by carrying towels, water, etc.

**Sample Adaptation of the Presidential Prayers for a Mass with Children**

*Opening Prayer*

Let us pray.

God our Father,
we gather together
just as Jesus did, at table with his friends,
the night before he died for us.
On that night Jesus handed over his life for us
and used bread and wine as signs of his love.
May Jesus, our Bread of Life,
fill us with his love
every time we gather at his table.
We ask this through Christ our Lord.

*Prayer over the Gifts*

Lord,
help us to be like Jesus,
as we gather at your table.

We remember that he gave his life for us;
may we receive again the gift of his love.
We ask this through Christ our Lord.
Amen.

*Prayer after Communion*
Let us pray.

Almighty God,
through sharing in this meal
you bring us closer to Jesus who gave us his Body and Blood.
Help us to live like Jesus
and to share with him for ever the feast of heaven.
We ask this through Christ our Lord.
Amen.

**Prayer of the Faithful for the Holy Thursday Mass with Children**
*Presider*
On this night,
when Jesus washed the feet of his friends,
as a sign of his love,
let us pray with love for people everywhere.

*Reader*
Let us pray for all the followers of Jesus: may they live like him by helping others.

(A response, sung or recited, may be added after each intention is proposed, or a pause for silent prayer may be observed.)

1. Let us pray for peace throughout the world: that people everywhere will learn to forgive their enemies.
2. Let us pray for all those who are sick: that God may make them better.
3. Let us pray for all of us who are gathered here tonight: that we may learn to think of others and find ways of being kind to them.

*Presider*
God our saviour,
you always love us.
Hear our prayers
and help us to love others.
We ask this through Christ our Lord.
Amen.

**Mass of the Lord's Supper: Texts of Readings adapted for Masses with Children**
(N = the part of the Narrator, + = the part of Christ)

*The Second Reading*
N. A reading from the first letter of St Paul to the Corinthians.

On the night that he was betrayed, the Lord Jesus took some bread, and thanked God for it and broke it, and he said,

+ 'This is my body, which is for you; do this as a memorial of me.'

N. In the same way he took the cup after supper, and said,

+ 'This cup is the new covenant in my blood. Whenever you drink it, do this as a memorial of me.'

N. Until the Lord comes, therefore, every time you eat this bread and drink this cup, you are proclaiming his death.

This is the word of the Lord.

*Gospel*
(If the Gospel is proclaimed within the setting of Mass, the part of Christ should be taken by an ordained minister. During a separate Liturgy of the Word for children it may be taken by another reader.)

N. A reading from the holy Gospel according to John.

All Glory to you, Lord.

N. Jesus got up from table, removed his outer garment and, taking a towel, wrapped it round his waist; he then poured water into a basin and began to wash the disciples' feet and to wipe them with the towel he was wearing.
When he had washed their feet and put on his clothes again he went back to the table. He said,

+ 'Do you understand what I have done to you? You call me Master and Lord, and rightly; so I am. If I then, the Lord and Master, have washed your feet, you should wash each other's feet. I have given you an example so that you may copy what I have done to you.'

N. This is the Gospel of the Lord.

All Praise to you, Lord Jesus Christ.

# MASS OF THE LORD'S SUPPER – SACRISTAN'S LIST

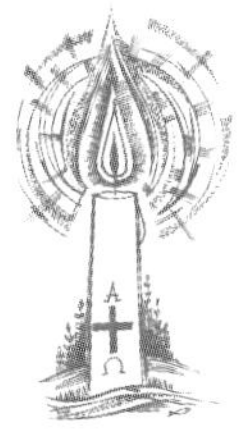

John McCann

**Sacristy**

- White vestments
- Cross
- Two processional candles, lighting
- Lighted thurible (and a second one for the eucharistic procession, if desired)
- Incense boat
- Presider's book (if it is going to be carried in by a server)
- Book of Gospels (unless it is put on the altar from before Mass)

**Sanctuary Area**

- Microphones checked: altar, ambo, chair
- Tabernacle empty
- Seating for servers
- Seating for concelebrants, if needed
- Chairs for candidates for the Washing of Feet in a suitable place
- If special gifts for the poor are to be brought up, an appropriate place needs to be found to accommodate them, preferably not in front of the altar or ambo.

**Ambo**

- Lectionary, marked

**Altar**

- Cloth and lighted candles
- Book of Gospels, if desired
- Microphone hidden behind the altar, if possible

**Credence Table**

- Missal, with pages marked. Instead of being located here, the Missal may be carried in the entrance procession from the sacristy by an altar server.
- Extra vessels for consecration, if needed (although it is better to bring up all the vessels for consecration in the procession with gifts)
- Chalice and purificator
- Extra chalices and purificators, if required for communion under both kinds
- Cruet of water
- Bowl and hand-towel
- Concelebration booklets, if desired

**Other table(s), suitably located**

- Jug, bowl and towels for washing of feet [warm water!]. Some scented oil in the water, if desired
- Bowl of warm water, soap and towel for the presider to wash his hands afterwards
- Sufficient space for the presider's chasuble
- Humeral veil
- Extra candles for those in the Blessed Sacrament procession (if desired) with a means of lighting them
- Sufficient charcoal

**Table for the Gifts to be Carried**

- It is preferable that all the bread and wine to be consecrated be carried in procession from this table.
- Remember to include enough bread to provide for tomorrow's liturgy.
- It can be effective to highlight the importance of the people's gifts by having a lighted candle on this table from before the beginning of Mass.

**Place of Reservation**

- The place to which the Blessed Sacrament will be transferred needs to be prepared in advance. When the ordinary tabernacle is located in a chapel separated from the central part of the church, this is an appropriate location to prepare the place of reservation.
- A tabernacle large enough to contain what is needed for the Good Friday Celebration is prepared in advance, and left open. This tabernacle should not be made to resemble a tomb or casket.
- The place of reservation is prepared in the same way as an altar, with cloth, corporal and lighted candles.
- The place of reservation would be prepared and adorned in such a way as to be conducive to prayer and meditation.

**Blessed Sacrament, Reserved**

- It may be necessary to have a secure place in the sacristy area where the Blessed Sacrament can be reserved temporarily (for example, so that the Eucharist is available for the dying during the day of Holy Thursday). A sanctuary lamp is lit at this location.

# MUSIC RESOURCES – MASS OF THE LORD'S SUPPER

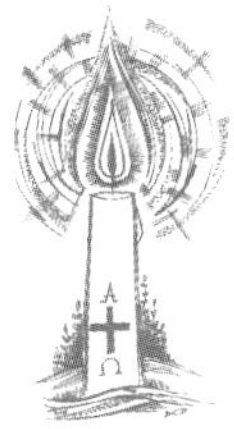

PAT O'DONOGHUE

**Entrance Song**
The purpose of the Entrance Song as indicated in the *General Instruction on the Roman Missal* is 'to open the celebration, intensify the unity of the gathered people, lead their thoughts to the mystery of the season or the feast, and accompany the procession of priest and ministers'.

The Entrance Antiphon is a useful source when choosing a suitable song:

> 'We should glory in the cross of our Lord Jesus Christ, for he is our salvation,
> Our life and resurrection; through him we are saved and made free.'

*We Should Glory* (Stephen Dean – *Easter Mysteries*), *The Glory of the Cross We Sing* (*The Great Week* – McCrimmon Publishing Company) and the *Per Crucem* (Taizé) follow this pattern. The sense of unity could be expressed in the hymn *Though So Many We Are One* (Paul Décha – *Alleluia Amen*) or in *We are his People* (Marty Haugen – *Gather*).

**Glory to God**
The following settings offer scope for the congregation to participate in the refrain.
*Glory to God* (Donal Hurley – *Seinn Alleluia 2000*)
*An Ghlóir* (Paul Nash – *Seinn Alleluia 2000*)
*An Ghlóir* (Liam Lawton – *Molaise*)
*Gloria* (Marty Haugen, Mass of Creation – *Gather*)

**Responsorial Psalm**
There are various settings of Psalm 115 in different styles available.
*Our Blessing Cup* (Marty Haugen – *Psalms for the Church Year 1*)
*Psalm 115* (*Responsorial Psalms of Holy Week* – Irish Institute of Pastoral Liturgy)
*Our Blessing Cup* (Stephen Dean – *The Great Week*)
*The Blessing Cup* (A. Gregory Murray OSB – *The Great Week*)

**Gospel Acclamation**
*Praise and Honour* (Stephen Dean – *The Great Week*)
*Glory and Praise* (Chris O'Hara – *The Great Week*)
*Praise to You* (Marty Haugen – *Gather*)

**The Washing of Feet**
A range of styles is available for this part of the liturgy.
*Servant Song* (Richard Gillard – *Hosanna*)
*The Lord Jesus* (Gregory Norbert – *Alleluia Amen*)
*Jesu, Jesu, Fill Us With Your Love* (Ghana Folk Song adapted by Tom Colvin – *The Great Week*)
*No Greater Love* (Michael Joncas – *The Great Week*)

**Preparation of Gifts**

*Ubi Caritas* is the anthem of the day and musical settings come in all styles.
Plainsong (*Seinn Alleluia 2000*)
Taizé (*Gather* or *In Caelo*)
*Where Charity and Love Are* (M. Cockett/ E. Welch – *In Caelo*)
*Where Charity and Love are Found* (John McCann – *In Caelo*)

**Eucharistic Prayer Acclamations**

These should be accessible to the assembly for full participation.
*Let Me Hear Your Voice* (John McCann – *Seinn Alleluia 2000*)
*Eucharistic Acclamations for Children* (Sue Furlong – *Seinn Alleluia 2000*)

**Communion Song**

There is usually time for a people's communion song and for a music-group piece.
*Let Us Be Bread* (Thomas J. Porter – *Seinn Alleluia 2000*)
*Mo Ghrá-sa Mo Dhia* (Liam Lawton – *Seinn Alleluia 2000*)
*We Remember* (Marty Haugen – *Gather*)
*A Íosa Mhilis* (Pat Ahern – *In Caelo*)
*Eat This Bread* (Taizé – *In Caelo*)
*Take and Eat* (Michael Joncas – *In Caelo*)
*We Give You Thanks* (David Haas – *In Caelo*)

**Procession to the Place of Repose**

*Pange Lingua/Hail Our Saviour's Glorious Body* (Plainchant – *Gather*)
*Of The Glorious Body Telling* (*The Great Week*)

# HOLY THURSDAY - HOUR OF PRAYER BEFORE THE BLESSED SACRAMENT

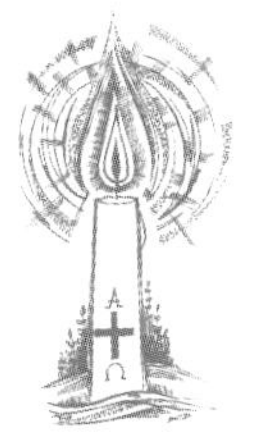

JOHN McCANN

This hour of prayer is divided into four quarters, each with its own focus. After the first section, which is about coming into the presence of Christ, each of the other sections develops themes found in the Eucharistic Prayer.[1]

*Opening Song*
*Stay Here and Keep Watch* (Taizé – *Gather*) or *Keep Watch With Me* (Margaret Rizza – *River of Peace,* Kevin Mayhew)

**1. Coming into the Presence of Christ**
*Reading*
As we gather together for prayer, let us listen to words written by Pope Paul VI, about the presence of Christ in the Eucharist:

'No one can fail to understand that the divine Eucharist bestows on the Christian people an incomparable dignity. Not only while the sacrifice is being offered and the sacrament has been received, as long as the Eucharist is kept in our churches and oratories, Christ is truly the Emmanuel, that is, 'God with us'. Day and night he is in our midst; full of grace and truth, he dwells with us. He forms our moral life, nourishes virtues, consoles the afflicted, strengthens the weak, moves all those who draw near to imitate him, learning from his example to be meek and humble of heart and to seek not what is their own but the things of God. Anyone, therefore, who approaches this august sacrament with special devotion and endeavours to return generous love for Christ's own infinite love, experiences and fully understands, with great spiritual joy and profit, how precious is the life hidden with Christ in God and how great is the value of communing with Christ, for there is nothing more consoling on earth, nothing more effective for advancing along the road of holiness.' (*Encyclical Mysterium fidei,* 67)

*Psalm*
Response: Come, let us adore the Lord, for he is our God.

Come, ring out our joy to the Lord;
hail the rock who saves us.
Let us come before him, giving thanks,
with songs let us hail the Lord. (R)

1. This is one of the structures used in the volume *Exposition and Benediction of the Blessed Sacrament,* published by the Irish Institute of Pastoral Liturgy, 1982.

A mighty God is the Lord,
a great king above all gods.
In his hand are the depths of the earth;
the heights of the mountains are his.
To him belongs the sea, for he made it,
and the dry land shaped by his hands. (R)

Come in, let us bow and bend low;
let us kneel before the God who made us
for he is our God and we
the people who belong to his pasture,
the flock that is led by his hand. (R)

*Glory be to the Father…*

*Song*
*Jesus Christ Yesterday Today and Forever* (Suzanne Toolan – *Seinn Alleluia 2000*)

*Silence*
Let us take a moment of silence to worship in the presence of the one who loved us and gave his life for us.

A pause for silent prayer is observed.

**2. Remembrance**
*Reading*
A reading from the first letter of St Paul to the Corinthians. (1 Cor 11:23-27)

This is what I received from the Lord, and in turn passed on to you: that on the same night that he was betrayed, the Lord Jesus took some bread, and thanked God for it and broke it, and he said, 'This is my body, which is for you; do this as a memorial of me.' In the same way he took the cup after supper, and said, 'This cup is the new covenant in my blood. Whenever you drink it, do this as a memorial of me.' Until the Lord comes, therefore, every time you eat this bread and drink this cup, you are proclaiming his death.
This is the word of the Lord.

All Thanks be to God.

*Reflection*
This evening our minds and hearts are drawn back to the Last Supper, when Jesus gave us the gift of the Eucharist. It was Passover time, that time of the year when the people recalled the great Exodus journey out of Egypt. At Passover time, the people remembered that moment way back in their early history when, by the hand of Moses, they were led from slavery to freedom, from sorrow to joy, from darkness to light, from shame to glory. They ate the Passover meal as a memorial of the wonderful way God had given them freedom. The Passover meal was a continual reminder of God's goodness, which would never fail them.

When Jesus shared the Last Supper with his disciples, he said, 'Do this as a memorial of me.' From now on, the great event they were to remember was his gift of himself on the cross. Jesus himself was the new Passover Lamb, given to us by God, sacrificed on the cross. Jesus made his great exodus journey from this world to the next. He has opened a way for us to walk the journey from sin to forgiveness, from death to life, from slavery to freedom. His body given and his blood shed are the enduring sign that no matter what place of suffering we may visit on our life's journey, Jesus has been there before us.

*Prayer of Remembrance*[2]
Jesus, saviour of the world,
at the last supper,
as you sat at table with your disciples,
you offered yourself as the spotless lamb,
a perfect gift for the whole of humanity.
You gave us this memorial of your passion
to bring us its saving power until the end of time.

Acclamation – My Lord and My God

In this great sacrament you feed your people
and strengthen them in holiness,
so that the family of humankind
may come to walk in the light of one faith,
in one communion of love.

Acclamation – My Lord and My God

You willingly gave yourself up to death
and taught us to make an offering in your memory.
As we eat your body given for us,
we grow in strength.
As we drink your blood poured out for us,
we are washed clean.

Acclamation – My Lord and My God

*Song*
*Mo Ghrá-sa Mo Dhia* (Liam Lawton – *Seinn Alleluia 2000*)

As we pause for silent prayer, let us remember all that Jesus has done for us.

A pause for silent prayer is observed.

**3. Thanksgiving**
*Reading*
A reading from the book of Exodus. (Ex 16:2-4, 13-15)

The whole community of the children of Israel began to complain against Moses and Aaron in the wilderness and said to them, 'Why did we not die at the Lord's hand in the land of Egypt, when we were able to sit down to pans of meat and could eat bread to our heart's content! As it is, you have brought us to this wilderness to starve this whole company to death!'

2. This prayer is an adaptation of materials found in the Prefaces of the Holy Eucharist given in the Missal.

Then the Lord said to Moses, 'Now I will rain down bread for you from the heavens. Each day the people are to go and gather the day's portion; I propose to test them in this way to see whether they will follow my law or not.'

And so it came about: quails flew up in the evening, and they covered the camp; in the morning there was a coating of dew all round the camp. When the coating of dew lifted, there on the surface of the desert was a thing delicate, powdery, as fine as hoarfrost on the ground. When they saw this, the children of Israel said to one another, 'What is that?' not knowing what it was. 'That' said Moses to them 'is the bread the Lord gives you to eat.'
This is the word of the Lord.

All Thanks be to God.

*Reflection*
The people of Israel were in fear for their lives. They faced starvation. They were afraid they would not survive the threat of the desert wastes. We too have our own fears about survival: Will I survive the loss of a loved one? Will I survive the stress of work or family life? Will I cope with the pains and humiliations of illness? When I die, will I survive? When we are faced with the threat of the desert or the howling wilderness, we need our own manna, our bread for the journey. We place our hopes in Jesus, who says, 'I am the true bread come down from heaven.' With him, we need not fear the journey into the unknown.

*Song*
*Be Not Afraid* (Bob Dufford – *Gather*)

*Litany of Thanksgiving*
Let us give thanks and praise to Christ, our living bread come down from heaven:

For the gift of your body and blood given in this sacrament.

R. We Praise You, O Lord.

For the sign of unity and the bond of peace given in this sacrament. R.

For the strength to follow your way and the joy to lighten the journey given in this sacrament. R.

For health to the sick and hope for sinners given in this sacrament. R.

For the pledge of eternal life and future glory given in this sacrament. R.

*Silence*

Let us continue to give thanks to God, each in our own way, in a short pause for silent prayer.

**4. Petition**
*Reading*
A reading from the holy Gospel according to Luke. (Lk 11: 9-13)

Jesus said to his disciples, 'Ask, and it will be given to you; search, and you will find; knock, and the door will be opened to you. For the one who asks always receives; the one who searches always finds; the one who knocks will always have the door opened to him. What father among you would hand his son a stone when he asked for bread? Or hand him a snake instead of a fish? Or hand him a scorpion if he asked for an egg? If you then, who are evil, know how to give your children what is good, how much more will the heavenly Father give the Holy Spirit to those who ask him!'

This is the Gospel of the Lord.

All Praise to you, Lord Jesus Christ.

*Intercessions*
For reconciliation and peace in our world, for harmony among nations and justice everywhere, let us pray to the Lord. A Thiarna, déan trócaire.

For the Church of God throughout the world, that he may give us peace and unity, let us pray to the Lord. A Thiarna, déan trócaire.

For the welfare of the sick, the care of those in need and the support of the lonely, let us pray to the Lord. A Thiarna, déan trócaire.

For the safety of travellers, the release of prisoners, and shelter for the homeless and exiled, we pray to the Lord. A Thiarna, déan trócaire.

For a holy and peaceful end to our lives, and for all those who have died in Christ, we pray to the Lord. A Thiarna, déan trócaire.

Lord Jesus, hear the prayers of your people
and be with us in all our needs.
Grant that we may receive
what we ask of you in faith.
Who live and reign for ever and ever.

All Amen.

*Song*
*Lord Increase our Faith* (David Haas)

*Concluding Prayer*
Lord our God,
in this great sacrament
we come into the presence of Jesus Christ, your Son,
born of the Virgin Mary
and crucified for our salvation.
May we who declare our faith in this fountain of love and mercy
drink from it the water of everlasting life.
We ask this through Christ our Lord.

All Amen.

# GOOD FRIDAY – WHAT'S GOOD ABOUT IT?

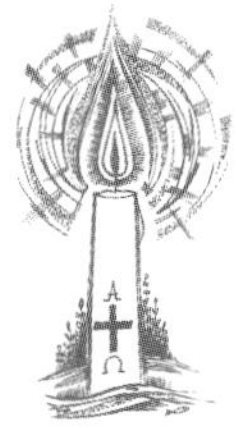

Pat O'Donoghue

**It is good to take time...**

Good Friday is still a public holiday in many countries. It is widely treated as yet another leisure holiday – a day for travelling, doing DIY, looking after spring gardening chores or shopping for the 'Easter holiday'. In Ireland the pubs are closed, but those who stock up in advance can beat the drought of the day. The variety of channels on TV offers a range of distractions from Sport to MTV, so that no one is bored by the enforced restrictions. This presents one picture of life at the beginning of the twenty-first century. At the same time more people are drawn to the liturgies of Good Friday than to the other days of the triduum – it is good to take time in planning this liturgy.

**It is good to be here...**

In the past, only solemn music was played on the radio and serious films were shown on television on this day. From noon to three o'clock a quietness settled over neighbourhoods as the Lord's Passion was commemorated. The nearest we came to recapturing that atmosphere in Ireland was the National Day of Mourning on 14 September 2001 to mark the unfolding tragedy in the United States of America. The churches were overflowing as people came to sign books of condolence, to reflect, to grieve and to pray for peace on the Feast of the Triumph of the Cross. This event and the earlier visit in 2001 of the Relics of St Thérèse of Lisieux indicate a willingness in people to gather when there is some opportunity to express their faith in a tangible way. The sense of touch is the common factor in many of these public expressions. The Veneration of the Cross is a central element in the liturgy of Good Friday and opportunities outside the main liturgy for this expression of respect and reverence should also be provided.

**It is good to be together...**

The Celebration of the Lord's Passion is the central liturgical act of the day. Ideally this liturgy should take place around 3.00 p.m., but for pastoral reasons another time between noon and 9.00 p.m. can be chosen to facilitate the gathering of the community. All other celebrations, such as the Way of the Cross, should flow into or from the main liturgical celebration and should combine the elements of passion with those of victory and the new life bought by the death of Jesus Christ.

> 'In contemplating the cross of its Lord and Bridegroom, the Church commemorates its own origin and its mission to extend to all peoples the blessed effects of Christ's passion that it celebrates on this day in a spirit of thanksgiving for this marvellous gift.'
>
> *Ceremonial of Bishops,* 312.

# GOOD FRIDAY - MORNING PRAYER

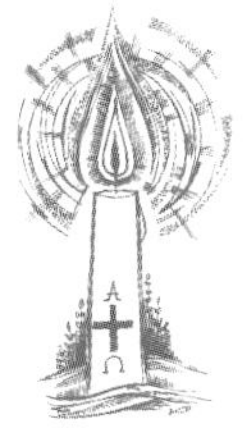

PAT O'DONOGHUE

It is recommended that the Office of Readings and Morning Prayer be celebrated publicly on this day. It would be important to have books or texts for the congregation to help them participate as fully as possible. As the assembly may be small in number you might like to gather them in a small space that is intimate. The cross for veneration at the later celebrations might be in place as a simple focus. Some people would like to join in the full celebration of the Office as in the Breviary. The following adjustments in an alternative style might help those unfamiliar with such a full celebration.

*Opening Hymn*
*Praise to the Holiest* (J. H. Newman/R. R. Terry – *Veritas Hymnal)*

*Psalm 21*
*My God, My God* (Marty Haugen – *Gather*)

All sing My God, my God, O why have you abandoned me?

*Psalm Prayer*
Gracious God, we unite our anxieties and our sense of abandonment with the lonely pain of Christ on the cross. Be with those who feel deserted and alone today. We ask this in the Spirit, through Christ our Lord. Amen.

*Reading*
Hebrews 9: 11-28
*Christ, the high priest, through the shedding of his own blood*
*has entered the sanctuary once and for all.*

*Psalm 50*
*Be Merciful O Lord* (Michael Joncas – *Gather*)

All sing Be merciful, O Lord, for we have sinned.

*Psalm Prayer*
Forgiving God, we are conscious that we have added our sins to those of all humanity. Grant us the reward of salvation for which we wait in joyful hope.
We ask this in the Spirit, through Christ our Lord. Amen.

*Reading*
Isaiah 52:13-15

*Antiphon*
Christ humbled himself for us and, in obedience, accepted death, even death on a cross.
*OR*
*Passion Meditation* (Chris Walker – *Music for the Mass 1*)

All sing For me, you gave up your life.

*Gospel Canticle*
*Benedictus*
Blessed be the Lord, the God of Israel!
He has visited his people and redeemed them.

He has raised up for us a mighty saviour
in the house of David his servant,
as he promised by the lips of holy men,
those who were his prophets from of old.

A saviour who would free us from our foes,
from the hands of all who hate us.
So his love for our fathers is fulfilled
and his holy covenant remembered.

He swore to Abraham our father to grant us,
that free from fear, and saved from the hands of our foes,
we might serve him in holiness and justice
all the days of our life in his presence.

As for you, little child,
you shall be called a prophet of God, the Most High.
You shall go ahead of the Lord
to prepare his ways before him,

To make known to his people their salvation
through forgiveness of all their sins,
the loving kindness of the heart of our God
who visits us like the dawn from on high.

He will give light to those in darkness,
those who dwell in the shadow of death,
and guide us into the way of peace.

Glory be to the Father, and to the Son, and to the Holy Spirit,
as it was in the beginning, is now and ever shall be,
world without end. Amen.

*Intercessions* (Breviary)

*Concluding Prayer* (Breviary)

All depart in silence.

# GOOD FRIDAY
# THE CELEBRATION OF THE LORD'S PASSION

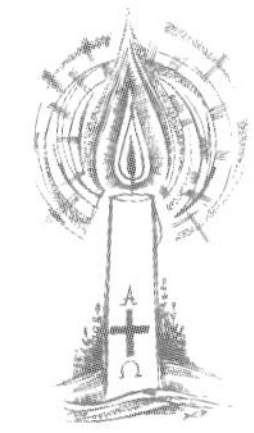

LIAM TRACEY

The Church gathers this afternoon in a paradoxical celebration. We celebrate the cross, an instrument of torture and death, as a place of revelation where the wondrous love of God for humanity shines out in the death of Jesus. This paradox must be held in our liturgical celebration today. The cross of Christ lies at the heart of our faith, and anyone who wishes to follow the path of Christ will sooner or later encounter the cross. Today's liturgy does not avoid the cross. It places it at the heart of the celebration where it is venerated as the instrument of salvation by the community of faith gathered. We kiss the wood of the cross, which has become the throne of the crucified one who passes through the reign of death, rises to life and sets us free. Our celebration leads us into prayerful intercession for the Church and the world.

**Rooted in the Triduum**

Any preparation for the celebration of Good Friday must root itself in the sweep of the three great days that reach their culmination in the celebration of the Easter Vigil. So our preparation must be done in conjunction with those who are preparing the celebration of the other days in order that the triduum is celebrated as a whole. There is no gathering rite or dismissal rite, a sign that the Church entered into the triduum on Holy Thursday and remains there, watching and keeping vigil. Our prayer goes on right over these days and those gathering for the liturgy are gathering up in a public way that prayer of our homes and places of work.

It is important to remember in the period of preparation for the triduum, that it is not about dramatising the events of the various days, but rather a celebration of the event of our salvation. The celebration of Good Friday is rooted in the paschal victory of Christ, who even today, and especially today, has conquered death and brought us to life. Any suggestion that Christ is crucified again or that we are left outside the providential care of God should be avoided.

The celebration of the Lord's Passion occupies a central place today. All other celebrations (Way of the Cross, etc.) and prayers flow from this celebration and into it. Therefore, in terms of time and preparation it takes priority, and other celebrations are arranged and prepared later. In their preparations, liturgy groups should use the liturgical books themselves and not rely on missalettes, which rarely provide all the options and rubrics. This practice will enable them to become comfortable in their use of the liturgical books.

**Settings and Preparation**

The space is stripped to its essentials: the bare table of the altar, an empty baptismal font, the ambo and the seating for the assembly (no candles lit at shrines, no holy water in the stoops). Only the *Sacramentary* is required from the beginning and red is the colour of the vestments for the celebration. Because of the many strong features of this celebration, careful thought has to go into the preparation: the best way to proclaim the passion, the veneration of the cross, how to proclaim the general intercessions, suitable song. This liturgy holds together in a simple but profound way the mystery of Easter: grief and sorrow, glory and life.

The liturgy begins in silence. All preparation should cease before the people gather, so that the setting is one of prayer and silence. While you can have an entrance procession with the presider and the other ministers, perhaps think about the presider and the other ministers taking their place in the assembly near the altar fifteen to twenty minutes before the liturgy begins. At the hour they can stand, and with them the whole assembly. Moving to the front of the altar they bow and then kneel. All present do the same. When all are kneeling, the ministers prostrate. This annual sign should last a couple of minutes and is a time for silent prayer – give it time and space. In some places the whole assembly may prostrate, if the space and furniture allow. There are no introductions or extra words of any kind today, the presider then recites or sings the prayer.

**The Proclamation of the Passion**

A central feature of the Good Friday liturgy is the proclamation of the passion according to John. In a sense this gives the liturgy its whole tone and shape. Jesus in the account of John is the King who ascends his throne, on the cross his glory is made manifest and his identity as the beloved one of God is shown to all the world.

The manner of the proclamation needs to be carefully considered by those preparing the liturgy today. Reducing the assembly to taking the parts of the crowd should be avoided, and if this option is in the missalette provided, it could be removed. Some parish communities intersperse the proclamation of the passion with singing at appropriate pauses. This needs careful preparation, clear instructions and suitable texts which clearly follow the unfolding of the Gospel narrative. A Taizé chant or something similar allows for a reflective acclamation and welcome of the Gospel message. This approach respects the text and its proclamation. The sung responses come at critical moments in the text, rather than as interruptions, which happens with the crowd parts. Singing an acclamation seems to be a more authentic response to the proclamation of the Gospel than shouting out responses, which reduces the worshipping assembly to a walk-on part in a passion play. In preparing for the proclamation of the Gospel a decision must also be made regarding the number of readers and, if there is more than one, how the text is to be divided among the readers. The best solution (one that is not always possible, but still to be aimed for over a number of years) is to have one reader. This person is someone who can proclaim the strength and mystery of the great account of John. This is someone who can lead us ever deeper into the familiar story and the words that shape our lives. If a number of readers is the solution arrived at by the preparation group, have the readers proclaim blocks of texts rather than take parts or characters in the Gospel account. The choice of the passion Gospel of John by the Church teaches us something crucial about the meaning of Good Friday; it is not a story told to leave us in despair or without hope. The cross is the glorification of Jesus, his shining forth to the world as the Beloved One of God.

The proclamation of the Gospel is not a passion play, nor should it attempt to be one. Today is a day for the assembly to be shaped and transformed by the experience of the cross; it is not about entertainment or even about evoking emotion. The movement of the Gospel today is towards the veneration of the cross.

The Liturgy of the Word (Isaiah 52:13-53:12, Psalm 30, Hebrews 4:14-16; 5:7-9 and John 18:1-19:42) is followed by a time of silence and the homily. It is not a good idea not to preach today; all the standard arguments, that the Gospel is rich enough, or of the length of time intruding on the silence of people, cannot escape the fact that it is the task of the homilist to link what we have just heard in the readings to the life of the community. That task cannot be neglected, especially today. The homily need not be long, but some well-chosen words on the whole liturgy can and will deepen the experience for many of the assembly.

**The General Intercessions**

The solemn prayers conclude the Liturgy of the Word. If the Word has been badly proclaimed, the homily long and tedious, or omitted, people can really start to feel bored at this point. If the Word has been well proclaimed and responded to, if the homily engaged with the mystery we celebrate, it seems logical that we now stand to intercede for the whole of creation. If the prayers of the faithful are done poorly Sunday after Sunday, chances are that they are not going to be done well today. The General Intercessions need to catch us in a sweep of prayer and intercession, that give the assembly a sense of their being about their priestly work, that their presence this afternoon is essential. Because of their structure, the call to prayer, silence and the prayer of the presider, there is a temptation to rush through them and not 'bore' the assembly. What is at issue is pace and a strength of proclamation by experienced readers who can catch us up in this sweep of prayer. If a deacon is not available to sing or say the introduction to the prayer, there really should be a woman's voice to complement the man's voice to conclude each intercession. The use of a sung acclamation after the presider's prayer, as provided for in the *Sacramentary*, can also be discussed by the preparation group.

**The Veneration of the Cross**

The climax of today's liturgy is the veneration of the cross. The origin of this tradition is more than likely in the fourth-century liturgy of the Church of Jerusalem; the bishop held the relic of the cross and the assembly came forward to touch it with their foreheads, with their eyes, and then they kissed it. This tradition of Jerusalem spread to other Churches. At first the veneration was of a relic of the true cross, later an image of the cross was used and still later the crucifix came into use.

Maybe this year you could spend some time reflecting on the cross that you use in your parish community. If the cross or crucifix that you use is visible to the assembly all through the year, then you do not need to change this practice. If, on the other hand, it is never seen except today, perhaps now is the time to change this. A wooden cross is the best choice and one that responds best to the images of the liturgy today. A simple wooden cross reflects the whole Paschal Mystery: dying you destroyed our death, rising you restored our life, Lord Jesus come in glory. The wood of the cross recalls the tree of life, the ark of Noah, the firewood prepared by Abraham, the staff of Moses. Images recall other images in this liturgy.

Only one cross should be used for the veneration, as indicated in the *Sacramentary*. If the number of people makes it impossible for everyone to venerate the cross individually, the priest may take the cross, after some of the faithful have venerated it, and stand in the centre in front of the altar. In a few words he invites the people to venerate the cross and then holds it up briefly for them to worship in silence. The cross can be venerated after the liturgy and again the next day.

**Communion**

The thrust of the Good Friday liturgy suggests that the communion rite should be a simple one. If there is singing during communion, it seems appropriate to repeat some of the music from Thursday; it should not, however, be a song that focuses on the bread and wine but perhaps on the cross. After the Amen of the assembly to the prayer, the celebration concludes in silence. The presider could just return to his place in the assembly and continue in silent prayer. The celebration does not conclude – we continue to watch and pray in vigil. The cross again becomes the centre of the worship area and should be easily approachable by the people. Perhaps burn some incense. As a people we begin to move towards the images of Holy Saturday, the day of rest, the day of burial; the Lord of life sleeps in the womb of the earth and we too enter into his rest. This needs to be kept in mind if an evening celebration is planned on Good Friday – it should respect the tone of the evening of Good Friday. This suggests that passion plays are not in keeping with the tone established. Prayer around the cross, or a watching and waiting liturgy, are more apt. None of these gatherings should, however, distract from or draw people away from the main celebration of the day.

# MUSIC RESOURCES
# THE CELEBRATION OF THE LORD'S PASSION

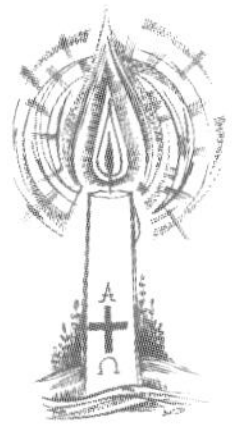

PAT O'DONOGHUE

As the procession enters in silence, the first musical possibilities are in the Liturgy of the Word.

**Responsorial Psalm – Psalm 30**
*The Great Week*
A Gregory Murray OSB
Stephen Dean
Fiona McArdle

*Gather*
David Haas
Marty Haugen

*Responsorial Psalms of Holy Week – IIPL*

**Gospel Acclamation**
Tony Barr – *The Great Week*
John Lillis – *The Great Week*
Any Lenten Acclamation + *Christ Was Humbler Yet* (Veritas)

**Intercessions**
A sung response is possible at this point and should be familiar to the congregation.

**Veneration of the Cross**
Apart from the *Roman Missal* chant in English or Latin, *The Great Week* offers three settings of the text for the procession. There are settings of the Reproaches available for the veneration: *The Great Week* offers two settings. Margaret Daly-Denton's setting was published by Veritas in 1993.

Songs of the Cross are also possible at this time:
*Gather*
*Crucem Tuam* (Taizé)
*Jesus The Lord* (Roc O'Connor)
*Behold The Wood* (Dan Schutte)
*All You Who Pass This Way* (Taizé)

**Communion**
The choices here follow the usual pattern for the selection of songs during communion.

# CELEBRATION OF THE LORD'S PASSION
# SACRISTAN'S LIST

JOHN McCANN

**In the Church**
- If possible, any crosses should have been removed from the church after the Thursday evening celebration. If they cannot be removed, they should be covered.
- Candles or lights should be removed from shrines.

**In the Sacristy**
- Red Mass vestments

**In a Convenient Place**
- A cross of size and beauty appropriate for veneration (veiled or unveiled, in purple or red, depending on the manner of veneration)
- Two candlesticks

**In the Sanctuary**
- The altar should be completely bare, without cloths, candles or cross.
- The *Roman Missal* in place for use at the presider's chair.
- Copies of the Lectionary and/or books for the reading of the Lord's Passion.
- If the Passion is to be read simultaneously by three readers, three microphones may be needed (if possible, avoid using the altar itself as a place of reading).
- On a side table: altar cloth, corporal, purificator(s) or other suitable cloth(s) for wiping the cross as needed.
- A suitable place needs to be found for placing the cross at the altar after it has been venerated. Some form of stand for the cross may need to be at hand.

**In the Place Where the Blessed Sacrament is Reserved**
- After midnight on Holy Thursday there is no solemn adoration at the place where the Blessed Sacrament is reserved. For this reason any decoration with flowers or extra candles should be removed. A single lamp burning is sufficient.
- Humeral veil
- Two candlesticks

# GOOD FRIDAY - A WAY OF THE CROSS

PAT O'DONOGHUE

This way of celebrating the Stations of the Cross gathers material from a variety of sources. The script draws from contemporary experiences of sadness and grief but also of victory and triumph. In addition, it uses traditional material and invites responses in word and music.

You can draw up your own script to suit your community by inviting a local creative-writing group to become involved in the project. Young people might also welcome the opportunity to shape a liturgy that creatively reflects their faith and uses multi-media facilities, at which they are often very adept. An important element is the participation of the preparatory group, who will work together over a period of time to draw out the various shades of meaning of the celebration of Good Friday and the Lord's Passion.

**Setting the Scene**
This liturgy can be celebrated at noon or in the evening if the Solemn Celebration of the Lord's Passion takes place in the afternoon. It is hoped that the texts will be accompanied by visual images of each Station, either on screen or by way of mime. The unadorned cross might be the central visual focus if no other imaging is possible. The use of music to help participation and to create the appropriate atmosphere should be restrained and sensitively chosen. Aromatherapy oils can be used to add to the atmosphere.

**Introduction**
A short explanation might be offered to the assembly and an invitation to participate extended to them. They should also be encouraged to embrace the opportunities for silence and reflection after each Station.

**Opening Song**
*The Clouds' Veil* (Liam Lawton – *In Caelo*)
Even though the rain hides the stars,
Even though the mist swirls the hills,
Even when the dark clouds veil the sky,
God is by my side.

Even when the sun shall fall in sleep,
Even when the sky shall weep,
Even when the storms shall rise,
God is by my side, you are by my side.

**First Station – Jesus is Condemned to Death**

Narrator

Throughout the world people are condemned to death every day for a range of offences from murder to robbery or for their political and religious affiliations. Human Rights organisations and various Church groups have worked to lobby for change. What can we do?

Voice 1

In Nigeria an Islamic court sentenced a pregnant woman to death by stoning for having premarital sex.

Voice 2

In the United States of America there is one execution on average every three days. Very often these executions affect minorities from particular ethnic and social backgrounds.

Voice 1

Kofi Annan, Secretary General of the United Nations and winner of the Nobel Prize for Peace in 2001, received 3.2 million signatures during the Jubilee Year campaign seeking an end to executions. In response he stated: 'The forfeiture of life is too absolute, too irreversible, for one human being to inflict it on another, even when backed by legal process'.

Voice 2

Pope John Paul II has often spoken out against capital punishment: 'The new evangelisation calls for followers of Christ who are unconditionally pro-life: who will acclaim, celebrate and serve the Gospel of life in every situation. A sign of hope is the increasing recognition that the dignity of human life must never be taken away, even in the case of someone who has done great evil. Modern society has the means of protecting itself, without definitively denying criminals the chance to reform'.

Narrator

The Sant'Egidio Community has conducted an international campaign against the death penalty and continues to offer support and encouragement to people condemned to death. You too can help their work.

Prayer

We condemn others to death by our silence and inaction or by our lust for revenge. Lord, help us with our human inclination to strike back and to look for violent retribution.

> Where there is offence, let us offer mercy;
> Where there is violence, let us show restraint;
> Where there is injustice, let us act for right.

**Second Station – Jesus is made to bear his Cross**

Narrator

Crosses are portrayed in different styles and designs. The Irish Church has contributed to this rich tradition. The penal crosses of the eighteenth and early nineteenth centuries offered courage to a persecuted people. They could look on the suffering of Christ and at the same time contemplate his glorious resurrection after such a death. Just as crosses come in various forms, they appear in our lives in a variety of ways and often 'not in single spies but in battalions'.

Litany of the Cross

| | |
|---|---|
| For the cross of infertility | Déan trócaire is trua |
| For the cross of stillbirth | Déan trócaire is trua |
| For the cross of infant death | Déan trócaire is trua |
| For the cross of handicap | Déan trócaire is trua |
| For the cross of neglect | Déan trócaire is trua |
| For the cross of discrimination | Déan trócaire is trua |
| For the cross of violence | Déan trócaire is trua |
| For the cross of war | Déan trócaire is trua |
| For the cross of terrorism | Déan trócaire is trua |
| For the cross of sickness | Déan trócaire is trua |
| For the cross of old age | Déan trócaire is trua |
| For the cross of terminal illness | Déan trócaire is trua |
| For the cross of injustice | Déan trócaire is trua |
| For the cross of famine | Déan trócaire is trua |
| For the cross of drought | Déan trócaire is trua |
| For the cross of isolation | Déan trócaire is trua |
| For the cross of alienation | Déan trócaire is trua |
| For the cross of marginalisation | Déan trócaire is trua |
| For the cross of addiction | Déan trócaire is trua |
| For the cross of mental illness | Déan trócaire is trua |
| For the cross of suicide | Déan trócaire is trua |
| For the cross of death through sickness | Déan trócaire is trua |
| For the cross of death by accident | Déan trócaire is trua |
| For the cross of death by violence | Déan trócaire is trua |
| For the cross of unemployment | Déan trócaire is trua |
| For the cross of homelessness | Déan trócaire is trua |
| For the cross of poverty | Déan trócaire is trua |

## Third Station – Jesus Falls the First Time

Testimony

'The AA programme was going so well for me. At last I had found people who understood me – people who had the same struggles with alcohol as I did. It's amazing how so many people from different backgrounds and education could end up the same way – cursed with addiction to alcohol. Not able to face life – even the simplest of tasks – without the crutch of alcohol. For years my wife, my family and my friends told me that I had a problem. It was only when I was near to losing my job that the penny dropped and I got help.

I was seven months dry when I went to a going-away party for one of the girls at work. I thought that I could just take one and that I could stop there. The addiction is like a silent enemy which is always lurking inside me. One glass of lager led to more, until I was legless again. I was so ashamed the next day – the disappointed faces of my kids, the hostility of my wife. I went to the lunchtime meeting and thankfully I was back on the dry again. The meeting gives me hope because I talk there to others in the same boat. I don't have that feeling of being outside as I used to – this is a place where I fit in because I am a recovering alcoholic. It is a year since I began the programme and my first fall was six months ago – keep me in your prayers.'

Serenity Prayer

God, grant me the serenity
To accept the things I cannot change,
Courage to change the things I can,
And the wisdom to know the difference.

Song

*Be Not Afraid* (Bob Dufford – *Gather*)

Be not afraid, I go before you always,
Come follow me, and I will give you rest.

You shall cross the barren desert
But you shall not die of thirst.
You shall wander far in safety
Though you do not know the way.
You shall speak your words in foreign lands
And all will understand.
You shall see the face of God and live.

Be not afraid, I go before you always,
Come follow me, and I will give you rest.

**Fourth Station – Jesus meets Mary, his Mother**

Narrator

People who have been close to death or who have been deeply shocked by some happening often describe how the events of their lives flashed before them in an instant. When Mary met her Son on his painful journey and as she stood by the cross her mind must have been drawn to the events of his short life. The Seven Sorrows of Mary and the Seven Joys of Mary offer a contrasting account of the life of Jesus and present the two aspects of the story of our salvation. These are spoken alternately by two readers.

1(a) The Virgin's first sorrow was
when her Child was hunted down,
black caps on the Jews and they beating him.

(R) Lord, have mercy *or* Kyrie eleison *or* A Thiarna, déan trócaire

1(b) The first joy the Blessed Virgin had,
wasn't it the great joy,
was the joy she had from her One Son Jesus
when she brought him into the world in a stable. (R)

2(a) The Virgin's second sorrow was
when her Child was hunted down,
a rough hairy shirt on him and his skin torn asunder. (R)

2(b) The second joy the Blessed Virgin had,
wasn't it the great joy,
was the joy she had from her One Son Jesus
when he walked with her upon the road. (R)

3(a) The Virgin's third sorrow was
when her Child was hunted down,
he on the cross of torment and the sharp nails tearing him. (R)

3(b) The third joy that the Blessed Virgin had,
wasn't it the great joy,
was the joy she had from her One Son Jesus
when he went reading his book. (R)

4(a) The Virgin's fourth sorrow was
when her Child was hunted down,
he on the tree of the cross winning graces for our souls. (R)

4(b) The fourth joy that the Blessed Virgin had,
wasn't it the great joy,
was the joy she had from her One Son Jesus
when he turned the water into beer. (R)

5(a) The Virgin's fifth sorrow was
when her Child was hunted down,
his head on the top of a spike spilling all his blood. (R)

5(b) The fifth joy that the Blessed Virgin had,
wasn't it the great joy,
was the joy she had from her One Son Jesus
when he made the dead come to life. (R)

6(a) The Virgin's sixth sorrow was
when her Child was hunted down,
he on her fair breast stretched out cold and dead. (R)

6(b) The sixth joy that the Blessed Virgin had,
wasn't it the great joy,
was the joy she had from her One Son Jesus
when with his blood he saved the world. (R)

7(a) The Virgin's seventh sorrow was
when her Child was hunted down
he stretched in the tomb and the flagstones across him. (R)

7(b) The seventh joy that the Blessed Virgin had,
wasn't it the great joy,
was the joy she had from her One Son Jesus
when he placed on her a crown. (R)

(*Saltair*, Des Forristal and Pádraig Ó Fiannachta)

**Fifth Station – Simon of Cyrene helps Jesus to carry his Cross**

Narrator

The members of the Simon Community undertake extraordinary work on behalf of the homeless. Through their mission and by their name they indicate how the story of Calvary can inspire people to action. We thank God for the many organisations and groups who help us to carry our cross in life.

Litany of Thanksgiving

| | |
|---|---|
| For the Society of St Vincent de Paul | We praise you, O God |
| For the Samaritans | We praise you, O God |
| For the Simon Community | We praise you, O God |
| | |
| For Focus Ireland | We praise you, O God |
| For Combat Poverty | We praise you, O God |
| For Aoibhneas | We praise you, O God |
| | |
| For Alcoholics Anonymous | We praise you, O God |
| For Gamblers Anonymous | We praise you, O God |
| For Narcotics Anonymous | We praise you, O God |
| | |
| For Childline | We praise you, O God |
| For Faoiseamh | We praise you, O God |
| For Amen | We praise you, O God |
| | |
| For Cura | We praise you, O God |
| For Victim Support | We praise you, O God |
| For the Rape Crisis Centre | We praise you, O God |
| | |
| For the Society of Simon of Cyrene | We praise you, O God |
| For Bethany Bereavement Groups | We praise you, O God |
| For Beginning Experience | We praise you, O God |
| | |
| For Trócaire | We praise you, O God |
| For Concern | We praise you, O God |
| For Goal | We praise you, O God |
| | |
| For Aware | We praise you, O God |
| For Recovery | We praise you, O God |
| For Grow | We praise you, O God |
| | |
| For the Irish Cancer Society | We praise you, O God |
| For the Alzheimer's Society | We praise you, O God |
| For the Irish Kidney Association | We praise you, O God |

**Sixth Station – Veronica wipes the face of Jesus**

Narrator

Artists have offered us their pictures of the face of Jesus over the past two thousand years. Early impressions give us the image of Christ as a sun-god, a shepherd and a law-giver. He is portrayed as a youthful man without a beard. In contrast, later representations of Christ gave him a certain gravitas and assigned to him the clothes of a secular ruler raised above and removed from his people.

Where is the face of Jesus to be seen today? The encounter with Veronica leaves us with the image of the suffering Jesus whose face is etched on those who are carrying their cross of pain and suffering today. The true icons of Jesus are presented to us on TV as we daily watch the torment of the victims of famine, war, pestilence and death.

Let us take some time to bring these uncomfortable images to mind now or to look at the pictures before us as we contemplate the face of Christ today.

Song
*Servant Song* (Richard Gillard – *Gather*)

Will you let me be your servant, let me be as Christ to you;
Pray that I may have the grace to let you be my servant too.

I will hold the Christ light for you in the night-time of your fear.
I will hold my hand out to you, speak the peace you long to hear.

I will weep when you are weeping, when you laugh I'll laugh with you.
I will share your joy and sorrow 'til we've seen this journey through.

**Seventh Station – Jesus Falls the Second Time**
Testimony
'I was in jail for stealing and using a credit card. I went on the detox programme. I was clean for the first time in three years. Through a contact at the shelter I got a job – money in my pocket and feeling good about myself. I thought that I had everything under control. I went with a few mates to a Disco in town. It was Hallowe'en and everyone was going wild. We had dressed up as Westlife and were the centre of attention. I noticed that Jason, one of the lads, was chatting with a guy who deals in cocaine. They disappeared to the toilets, and even though I knew what they were at I had to go too. I just didn't think. I was on a high with all the attention, the music, the buzz. So I snorted for the first time in a year. My girlfriend nearly freaked when she found out and saw the state of me. I was a sorry guy the next day.

I thought – that's it now. I was marched back to my sponsor on the drug programme by she who must be obeyed. Half of me resented being bossed around. In the end I knew that if I slipped up on a regular basis I would find myself back where I was before.

The good resolution lasted about two months and then the next temptation came along. We were going to a gig in town. I was tired. I had been having a hard time from my boss. My mother was on my case about the state of my room and not giving her enough money. The girlfriend wanted to know where I was all the time. So I broke loose and went to the gig. They were passing Es around. I said no to the first two approaches. Then I said – I've had enough. I took two and was flying. The music was the sweetest I had ever heard. The downer and the thirst were killing me later. I ran into my ma when I got home. You see she had been through the programme and she knew all the signs to watch out for. There was hell to pay. Facing my sponsor the second time after all my promises was one of the lowest times in my life.

I'm clean again but I am wiser. I am not saying that it will never happen again but I am stronger because someone believes in me and is there when I fall. I am not on my own. I am not very religious but I light a candle every day on my way to work. I carry a small wooden disc in my pocket. I take it with me everywhere. I even take it with my football gear. When I am tempted I have only to touch it and it helps me and reminds me of what I should do. I like Good Friday – it is my day in the year. I watch the kids dressing up for the play in the church – the soldiers, the crowd and Jesus and the cross. I say to myself – he knows what it is like to suffer, he is the one who is there for me.'

The Cross in my Pocket
I carry the cross in my pocket to remind me of who I can be,
if I take up my cross and I follow wherever my Saviour leads me.

Song
*Be Not Afraid* (Bob Dufford)

Be not afraid, I go before you always,
Come follow me, and I will give you rest.

**Eighth Station – Jesus Speaks to the Women of Jerusalem**
Narrator
These women remind us of the common humanity in which we all share.

'Weep not for me,' Jesus said, 'but for yourselves and for your children.'

Weep for the sickness, for the falsehood, for the exploitation of yourselves by yourselves, weep for the injustice. Weep for the delaying of the reign of God, not on earth as it is in heaven. Weep for the failure of your own unbelief, for the weakness and shallowness that you find even in the Church. Jesus came that He might bring all of this to an end, yet our response is to make an end of Him, whether by compromise, by false kindness, or by rejection.

Dear Lord, we are your people and we know that You love us. We know the sadness of our own tears only too well. We are told that on one occasion You wept for the city of Jerusalem, and that You spoke of a mother-hen wanting to gather her chicks under her wings. Give us a sense of those wings, and let us know Your warmth as You gather us now into the reign of God upon earth.
(Maurice Reidy, *Lourdes Pilgrim's Handbook* – Dublin Diocesan Pilgrimage)

**Ninth Station – Jesus Falls a Third Time**
Testimony
'This Station reminds me of a horse that I thought was a dead certainty. He was well backed for Cheltenham and fell at the last fence. He was in the last bunch at Aintree and a loose horse toppled him. The last straw was when he fell at Fairyhouse on Easter Monday. I got great odds for him with his recent history – I was already spending the money – well, paying back would be more truthful. Not for the first time did I go home with my tail between my legs wondering how I would explain to him where the housekeeping money had gone.

I have been in Gamblers Anonymous for years. After a few shaky starts I never miss a meeting and thank God my family life is fairly normal again.

You probably think that women are only addicted to one-arm bandits. I would bet literally on two flies going up the wall. In the process I have put my family through hell. You see they didn't realise for ages that I could not be trusted with money. I had excuses for everything and I could juggle my debts like the Minister for Finance balances the budget.

I had promised all and sundry that I would not gamble again. People don't know the pressure that Christmas puts on a family with a small income. Or the expectations of kids today for the best in Communion and Confirmation clothes. It was the Scratch Cards that did it. I am like your woman on the radio ad. who had to retire from wrist strain. One more and I would get the jackpot. Instead of the big scoop, like the horse I fell again. But this time I had the experience of the meetings and the ready support of a great group of people. It wasn't easy facing the shame of falling again. I didn't stay down though and now I am taking each day as it comes. I'm thankful for what I have and that in wasting so much money I didn't lose the family that mean so much to me.'

Song
*Be Not Afraid* (Bob Dufford)

> Be not afraid, I go before you always,
> Come follow me, and I will give you rest.

If you pass through raging waters
In the sea, you shall not drown.
If you walk amid the burning flames,
You shall not be harmed.
If you stand before the power of hell
And death is at your side,
Know that I am with you through it all.

> Be not afraid, I go before you always,
> Come follow me, and I will give you rest.

**Tenth Station – Jesus is Stripped of his Garments**

Narrator
Sickness is the great leveller. Standing before the doctor or lying in a hospital bed there may be some cosmetic differences between people but essentially we are stripped of all that gives us status and position in the world. We are vulnerable, sensitive and fragile. This is especially true for those who are dying. They try to read the expressions of family, friends and doctors, looking for confirmation of their worst fears. This experience puts us in touch with the isolation and humiliation of Jesus at this point in his suffering journey. Let us be sensitive then to those who are ill and give them the reassurance they need by our visits, our honesty and our embrace. Let us remember the sick and dying today and cover their fragility with the cloak of our prayers.

Intercessions
For those who are sick at home or in hospital, that the healing hand of the Lord may ease their pain, calm their fears and give them hope.

> We ask you, O God.

For those who care for the sick, that they may show them the dignity and respect they deserve in their time of trial.

> We ask you, O God.

For those close to death, that Christ may hold their hands and lead them to the joy of his kingdom.

> We ask you, O God.

**Eleventh Station – Jesus is Nailed to the Cross**

Narrator

Jesus was nailed to the cross as a final act of torture. Torture is prevalent today. Amnesty International reports that torture is inflicted on men, women and children in more than half the countries of the world.

They report further:

- Torture is still used to extract confessions, to interrogate, to punish or to intimidate.
- Torture even damages and distorts the hopes of future generations.
- Torture is neither inevitable nor natural.

Groups such as Amnesty International lobby political leaders and work to draw the attention of the people to such human rights violations. Powered with this information on the cruel oppression of people throughout the world today, we are called to respond with energy and conviction. Because this may not be happening in our country, we cannot pass by and ignore the pain of so many. We are their voice in the world today. What would Christ do in the circumstances?

Song

*Jesus Remember Me* (Taizé)

Jesus, remember me when you come into your kingdom.
Jesus, remember me when you come into your kingdom.

**Twelfth Station – Jesus Dies on the Cross**

Narrator

The death of Jesus on the cross of love was the supreme sacrifice. Every time we celebrate the Eucharist we participate in the sacrifice of Christ on the cross of love. From the history of the early Church we learn that the martyrs always found a way to celebrate the Eucharist.

> 'Every place we suffered became for us a place to celebrate… whether it was a field, a desert, a ship, an inn, a prison…'
>
> (Eusebius of Caesarea, *Historia Ecclesiastica VII,* 22, 4: 687-688)

Our ancestors in Ireland risked their lives in Penal Days to be present at the Eucharist. The Mass Rocks around this country tell a tale of faithfulness and love.

Cardinal Francis Xavier Van Thuan, who was made President of the Pontifical Council for Justice and Peace in 1998, was imprisoned in 1975 by the communist authorities in South Vietnam. He spent thirteen years in prison, nine of them in solitary confinement. The Eucharist was central to his life and he managed to celebrate Mass each day with small drops of wine given to him as medicine and some hosts that were smuggled into his cell. This is his story:

> 'Each time I celebrated Mass, I had the opportunity to extend my hands and nail myself to the cross with Jesus, to drink with him the bitter chalice. Each day in reciting the words of consecration, I confirmed with all my heart and soul a new pact, an eternal pact between Jesus and me through his blood mixed with mine. Those were the most beautiful Masses of my life.'
>
> (*Testimony of Hope*, Francis X. Van Thuan, Pauline Books and Media)

Prayer
Jesus, Bread of Life, give me a hunger for justice and peace.
Jesus, Bread of Life, nourish me that I may nourish others.
Jesus, Bread of Life, may I become more like you.

Jesus, Cup of Hope, give me a thirst for truth and honesty.
Jesus, Cup of Hope, fill me with your life-giving energy.
Jesus, Cup of Hope, pour your love into my heart.

**Thirteenth Station – The Body of Jesus is taken down from the Cross**

Narrator

Artists have attempted to capture the moment of sadness as the body of Jesus rests in the arms of his Mother. That expression of poignant love is a sign of the bond between our Saviour and the one whose 'yes' made possible our salvation. As Mary stood by the cross she also stood by the disciples of her Son and was with the Twelve when the Church was born on Pentecost.

We join in her song of praise – the Magnificat.
(Howard Hughes, *Seinn Alleluia 2000;* Dominican – *In Caelo*)

**Fourteenth Station – The Body of Jesus is laid in the Tomb**

Narrator

The entry of the body of Jesus into the tomb of sadness that first Good Friday became the place from which the glory of the Resurrection was proclaimed after three days. This is the hope that sustains us on our Christian journey and is the reason for our belief that those who have died in Christ will rise with him also in glory. We now remember those who have died at the Cross of Salvation and pray that they will be rewarded with the joyful vision of Christ for all time.

Together we pray the words of the Preface of Christian Death I:

> In him, who rose from the dead,
> Our hope of resurrection dawned.
> The sadness of death gives way
> To the bright promise of immortality.
>
> Lord, for your faithful people life is changed, not ended.
> When the body of our earthly dwelling lies in death
> We gain an everlasting dwelling place in heaven.

All come forward to venerate the cross while gentle music is played or sung.

Song
*Behold The Wood* (Dan Schutte – *Gather*)

Behold, behold the wood of the cross,
On which is sung our salvation.
O come, let us adore.

This Way of the Cross may be broken up into sections and used during Lent to prepare a group for the liturgy of Good Friday. It might also be used in the same way on the Fridays of Lent for those who want to follow a cross-centred journey during the season. It is envisaged that dramatised Stations may form the visual element of this celebration, or other media such as slides, video or pictures might be used. Local communities might adapt the texts to their situations and available music resources will determine what is sung or played. Supplies of the Cross in My Pocket (Wooden Disc) are available from the LitMus Office, Holy Cross College, Clonliffe, Dublin 3 – Tel 01 8571648 or Email *pdod@eircom.net.*

# GOOD FRIDAY
# SCRIPTURAL STATIONS OF THE CROSS

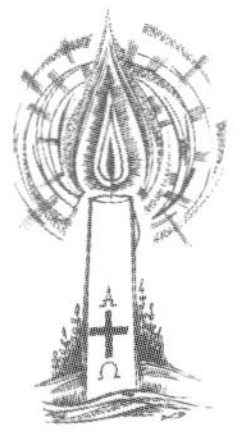

JOHN McCANN

Those who make pilgrimages to the Holy Land do so in order to visit the places made holy by the earthly journey of Jesus among us. They want to 'follow in his footsteps'. The idea of the Stations of the Cross arose in the Middle Ages as a kind of 'pilgrimage' at home, where we trace again the last moments of Jesus leading up to his death. Over the centuries the titles and number of Stations have varied. The traditional fourteen Stations that are found in almost every Catholic church or chapel were fixed in the eighteenth century.

In recent times further experimentation with the Stations has taken place. The Stations in Lourdes, for example, include a fifteenth Station of the Resurrection. With the growth of our appreciation of sacred scripture as the living word of God, versions of the Stations that are more firmly rooted in scripture have also been used. Some of the traditional fourteen come from tradition rather than scripture (for example, the three falls of Jesus; Veronica wipes the face of Jesus). These can be replaced by other Stations, or indeed the whole list can be reworked.

At the annual Stations of the Cross at the Colosseum in Rome, Pope John Paul II uses the following:

- Jesus prays in the Garden of Olives
- Jesus is betrayed by Judas
- Jesus is condemned to death by the Sanhedrin
- Jesus is denied by Peter
- Jesus is judged by Pilate
- Jesus is flogged and crowned with thorns
- Jesus carries his cross
- Jesus is helped by Simon of Cyrene
- Jesus encounters the women of Jerusalem
- Jesus is crucified
- Jesus promises to share his reign with the good thief
- Jesus is on the cross, with his mother and disciple below
- Jesus dies on the cross
- Jesus is placed in the tomb

These Stations draw on more than one Gospel. Another approach might be to take the Passion reading given for Passion Sunday of the particular year (Matthew, Mark or Luke) and work out which are the particular emphases of the evangelist in question. This could then form the basis of a new set of Stations, which would give something of the particular 'flavour' of each evangelist.

# GOOD FRIDAY
# LITURGY OF COMPASSION AROUND THE CROSS

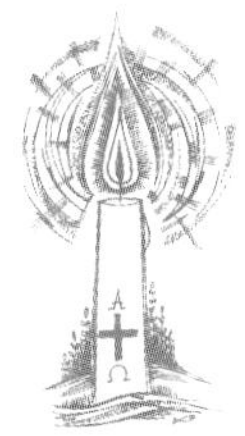

PAT O'DONOGHUE

*This liturgy can be used in Lent or during Holy Week by way of preparation for Good Friday. It is based on the Liturgy for Carers prepared for World Day of The Sick 2002.*

One group who beautifully illustrate the selflessness of Christ in his death and the power of his resurrection are the carers in our community. They tend and minister, often with little support or relief. They show by their lives the love of Christ on the cross and point to the victory of his sacrifice over death itself. No situation is so dark, no instance so stark that cannot in some way be touched by the light of Christ's love.

**Care and Caring in Ireland**

> In Ireland today, families are the prime care-givers. We know for example that only 5% of older people are institutionalised. The vast majority live at home. On the whole, they are well and independent. A number, however, need care and companionship. In addition, many chronically ill and disabled people are cared for full-time at home. It is estimated that there are approximately 100,000 informal carers in Ireland at present; 66,000 of whom care for older dependent relatives.
>
> *Circle of Care,* p. 74

**Preparation**

You might bring together a number of people who would help to focus the liturgy. Invite representatives of the caring professions, the statutory bodies and particularly carers to an exploratory meeting. Open the meeting to representatives of other faiths where applicable. Let those with a skill in planning liturgy listen to the reflections and input of those gathered. Let a small planning group shape the liturgy and allow for them to check in with members of the initial group to ensure that what is planned is faithful to their discussion and experiences. Invite all the carers in the community to the liturgy and organise volunteers to take their place for the duration. Incorporate some social event which will take place after Easter so that they might a have real sense of looking forward to a break from what they do so loyally every day. Let the wider community know what is happening and enlist help at a practical level.

**Location**

The number who are expected to attend will determine the space. A large church may be unsuitable whereas a small convent oratory might be the perfect place. Let the space indicate the warmth of support for carers, and perhaps by arranging the seating in a circle this can be further reflected. The centrepiece of the cross helps gather the attention of all for such a service. Surround the cross with candles or use the candles in a circle around the assembly to cast interesting shadows into the space. Let the scent of some healing oil add to the atmosphere. Aim for a feeling of relaxation and relief for weary people.

**Liturgy**

A gentle opening song like *Lord of All Hopefulness* or *Be Not Afraid* can be used by way of introducing a brief gathering rite. A vessel with oil is carried in and placed on a table close to the cross. A welcome and brief outline of the ceremony will help put people at their ease. Encourage those present to use the pauses for quiet reflection throughout the liturgy, which is structured on the model of Evening Prayer.

*Opening Prayer*
Let us pray,
Gentle Carer of our souls,
We lift up to you those who care for others.
As they follow your example on the cross of selfless giving,
May they know your support in difficult times
And be touched by your love for them.
We ask this through Christ, our Lord. Amen.

Then follows a pause for reflection as people sit and listen to an instrumental.

*Psalm of Intercession*
*Psalm 91* (Marty Haugen)

All sing Be with me, Lord, when I am in trouble.
Be with me, Lord, I pray.

*Psalm Prayer*
God, our Creator,
You gave us Jesus as our Saviour.
May he lift up those who are bowed down today
And carry them on eagles' wings.
May they know your strength and power.
We ask this through Christ, our Lord. Amen.

Pause for silent reflection

*Psalm of Comfort*
*Psalm 34* (Liam Lawton)

All sing The Lord will heal the broken heart.
God will seek the lost and find them.

*Psalm Prayer*
God, our Comforter,
You know our need for rest and support.
Heal hearts that are aching today,
Soothe the pain of weary hands
And give peace to troubled minds.
We ask this through Christ, our Lord. Amen.

Pause for silent reflection

*Song of Solidarity*
*Where Charity and Love* (John McCann)

All sing Where charity and love are found, there is God. *Repeat line*

Pause for silent reflection

*Reading*
Matthew 25:34-40

*Just as you did it to one of the least of these who are members of my family, you did it to me.*

*Address*

Some words of prayerful insight are offered to all present. Time for reflection follows while *Healer of My Soul* (John Michael Talbot) is sung.

*Litany of the Carer*
All stand and pray:

| | |
|---|---|
| For the helping hand | We thank you, O Lord |
| For the listening ear | We thank you, O Lord |
| For the gentle touch | We thank you, O Lord |
| For the sensitive word | We thank you, O Lord |
| For the card of support | We thank you, O Lord |
| For the bunch of flowers | We thank you, O Lord |
| For the spiritual gifts | We thank you, O Lord |
| For the professional help | We thank you, O Lord |
| For the voluntary services | We thank you, O Lord |

*Blessing of Hands*
The carers come forward and venerate the cross. They are then offered a blessing of hands with the healing oil.

Lord, bless these hands who lift, carry, wash and soothe.
Give them your healing touch and may they be gentle
As they comfort and help you in their sick brothers and sisters.
May your triumph on the cross give them hope and strength.
We ask this in the name of Jesus the Lord. Amen.

*Poem of the Carer*
That bell again,
Calling me to attention.
I am no sainted religious
Who moves obediently to prayer.

Patience etches itself on my face
Trying not to show impatience.

Aching limbs meet helplessness.
Nostrils twitch with pungent familiarity.

I curse my lot and long for the indifference
Of easy conscience and ready excuse to be excused.
The little irritations push me over
The threshold of endurance.

And then I think of you
With your arms outstretched for me
And you lift me up to see helping hands
And your mother's prayers rising up
Willing to make it better, and I accept.

*Song of Thanksgiving*
*Magnificat* (Dominican)

All sing Magnificat, Magnificat, anima mea Dominum.
Magnificat, Magnificat, anima mea Dominum.

*Concluding Prayer*
Gentle and Healing Lord,
Stay with us now and always.
Keep us and all those we care for in your tender love.
Give us strength when we despair,
And help when we need it most.
We ask this in Jesus the Lord. Amen.

Each person is given a spring bulb of hope, which is blessed while all sing together the final piece, *Ag Críost an Síol.*

Music suggestions are taken from *In Caelo* (Veritas 1999).

# LITURGY OF RECONCILIATION AROUND THE CROSS

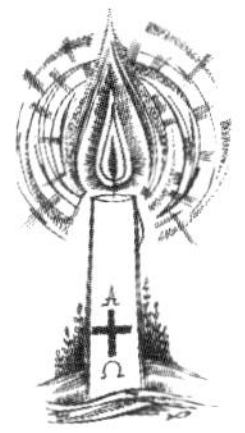

PAT O'DONOGHUE

**Setting the Scene**
Creating a prayerful atmosphere is an important part of this kind of liturgy. Reduced lighting, use of candles and the wooden cross laid flat on the floor or raised up as an icon are important elements.

As people arrive they should be welcomed and invited to take their place at their own discretion and given a participation sheet. Quiet, reflective music can be played to warm the space and to suggest quiet and reverence from the outset.

**Gathering Song**
A gathering song such as *Jesus Remember Me* (Taizé) will bring us directly to the foot of the cross and open us to the spirit of reconciliation. Gentle instrumental accompaniment will ease the burden of singing and can be alternated with voices.

**Greeting and Opening Prayer**
In the name of the Father of graces,
and of the Son who died for us,
and of the Spirit of courage and wisdom. Amen.

We gather around the cross of glory offering expressions of praise.
We bow our heads at the foot of the cross as a humble sign of thanksgiving.
We lift our eyes to the heavens, seeking reconciliation and healing.

**Reflection in Song**
John Michael Talbot's *Healer Of My Soul* (*In Caelo*) would be appropriate at this time, followed by a period of silence.

**Reading**
As Philippians 2:6-11 is read slowly, the setting of that text by Chris Walker (*Music for the Mass,* Book 1) is played and all then respond with the refrain – *For me you gave up your life.*

**Reflection on the Life of Blessed Columba Marmion**
Mark Tierney OSB has written *A Short Biography,* published by Columba Press, which would be an excellent source for a brief reflection. The following extract in the words of the Abbot might be useful on this occasion.

When I had finished my course of Philosophy, I was inclined to think of God rather as a tyrant. But one day, as I was praying at the foot of the Cross, Our Lord seemed to say to me: 'No greater love can a man have'. And then He seemed to add: 'The Father and I are One. That love of mine is a reflection of My Father'. From that moment on, I always visualised God as Love.

**Responsorial Psalm**
Liam Lawton's setting of Psalm 34, *The Lord Will Heal The Broken Heart* (*In Caelo*), could then be sung.

**Reading**
Luke 9:22

'The Son of Man', he said, 'is destined to suffer grievously, to be rejected by the elders and chief priests and scribes and to be put to death, and to be raised up on the third day.'

Then to all he said, 'If anyone wants to be a follower of mine, let him renounce himself and take up his cross and follow me. For anyone who wants to save his life will lose it; but anyone who loses his life for my sake, that man will save it. What gain, then, is it, for a man to have won the whole world and to have lost or ruined his very self? For if anyone is ashamed of me and of my words, of him the Son of Man will be ashamed when he comes in his glory and in the glory of the Father and the holy angels.'

**Words of Encouragement**
We are gathered around the cross of Jesus Christ with contrite hearts, trying to become more aware of what we have done and what we have failed to do. Our neglect or our deliberate actions, thoughts and words have contributed to the toll of sins for which Jesus died on the cross. We are here in a spirit of reconciliation to ask forgiveness for our neglect of Christ's call to complete selflessness and for running away from our responsibilities as his followers by not embracing the cross of humanity around us.

May the spirit of truth and honesty help us as we prepare to accept your gift of healing. May a spirit of humility enable us to recognise our pride, our self-righteousness and our tendency to judge others. May we also be committed to a change of heart and action as we try to build your kingdom here and now – a kingdom of justice, truth, love and peace.

We ask this through Jesus Christ, who is Lord yesterday, today and forever. Amen.

**Song of Mercy**
*Your Mercy Like Rain* (R. Cooney – *Seinn Alleluia 2000*)

Then follows an admission of sin in eight areas of our lives. We ask for forgiveness at each stage and resolve as Christian people to change our ways.

As each sin is announced, a large nail is carried forward and placed near the cross.

**I Sin Against Human Life**
Reader Let us pray that as members of the Christian community we may appreciate the damage, pain and suffering that result from our failure to defend human life at all moments from conception to death.

All say Lord, giver of all life, we see your face in the face of Christ, through whom you invite us to share in a relationship of love. We lament the sins of abortion and of euthanasia. We regret our neglect of the campaign to abolish the death penalty throughout the world. For these sins we ask your pardon and merciful forgiveness.

Pause

Presider Accept our resolve as a Church always and everywhere to be people of light and hope. May we always live to proclaim your Son, who came for the life of the world. We ask this through Jesus Christ, who offers everlasting life yesterday, today and forever.

Response Amen.

All sing Kyrie, Kyrie, Kyrie eleison

**II Sin Against the Dignity of Women**

Reader Let us recall the ways in which we have failed as a Church to acknowledge and recognise the goodness, talents and dedication of women in bringing to life the good news of salvation.

All say Loving and gracious God, you care for us with a mother's love: tender, compassionate and ever forgiving. You gave us Mary, the Mother of your Son, as an icon for all times. She was present at the foot of the cross as Jesus died for us. She was there with the apostles at the foundation of the Church at Pentecost. We lament the pain and suffering that women have felt over the years by the lack of recognition and respect for their dignity as one with men in Christ and heirs as well to the kingdom. For these sins we ask your pardon and merciful forgiveness.

Pause

Presider Accept our resolve as a Church to recognise always the dignity and giftedness of women. May we work together so that soon we might minister as one human family in the love of your Son. We ask this through Christ Jesus our Lord, yesterday, today and forever.

Response Amen.

All sing Kyrie, Kyrie, Kyrie eleison

**III Sin Against the Travelling Community**

Reader Let us pray that each one of us will recognise and appreciate the dignity and identity of the Travelling Community. Where this has not been the case, Travellers have been prevented from real participation in many aspects of society. They have suffered discrimination as a result of racism and prejudice. Their children are often excluded from activities that are taken for granted by the settled community. They are regularly judged negatively because of the actions and behaviour of a minority.

All say Lord, God of all tribes, cultures and nations, in spreading the good news of your Son, we have not always recognised or valued how you continually reveal yourself to people of every time and identity. We lament the ways we have failed to treat Travellers with respect, for our superior manner, our cultural insensitivity and our failure to honour their unique customs. For these sins we ask your pardon and merciful forgiveness.

Pause

Presider Accept our resolve as a Church to promote an appreciation and respect for the dignity of the Travelling Community by the way we live and interact with them. We ask this through the one true healer, Jesus Christ, yesterday, today and forever.

Response Amen.

All sing Kyrie, Kyrie, Kyrie eleison

**IV Sin Against Creation**
Reader Let us pray in thanksgiving for the gift and wonder of creation, for the land, the sea, the air and the stars. We have sought to conquer and harness the resources of this world for immediate and short-term goals. In neglecting to be fair stewards of God's gracious creation we forget that we do not inherit the earth from our ancestors but, rather, we borrow it from our children.

All say God of all creation, you have given us responsibility for this magnificent portion of your creation. And yet we have often failed to care for the environment and its resources. We lament our failure to respond, as a Church, to the awesomeness of your gifts by defending them from all who would defile them. For these sins we ask your pardon and merciful forgiveness.

Pause

Presider Accept our resolve as a Church to protect our environment and all of God's creation. Let us not bc wasteful and selfish in our use of these gifts but let us be active in ensuring a fairness of access to all people by our fair stewardship of creation. May we always hold in awe the wonder of your gifts. We ask this, through Jesus Christ, creator of all, yesterday, today and forever.

Response Amen.

All sing: Kyrie, Kyrie, Kyrie eleison

**V Sin Against New Immigrants to Our Country**
Reader Let us acknowledge the ways we have failed to welcome strangers into our communities, particularly immigrants, refugees and asylum-seekers who have come to live among us. As our people were welcomed in other lands, let us return that hospitality by our graciousness and welcome.

All pray God of our ancestors, we now have people of many nationalities and cultures among us. Calm our fear, inform our ignorance and open our eyes to your presence in those who have travelled to our shores. We lament our lack of hospitality and our failure to accept with helping hands our new neighbours from many lands. For these sins we ask your pardon and merciful forgiveness.

Pause

Presider Accept our resolve as a Church to open our hearts, our doors and our communities of faith to those who come among us as immigrants. We pray that we may value and esteem their presence, their culture and their talents. We ask this through Jesus Christ, king of all nations, yesterday, today and forever.

Response Amen.

All sing Kyrie, Kyrie, Kyrie eleison

**VI Sin Against the Rights and Dignity of Persons**

Reader Let us acknowledge our failure to recognise and defend the basic rights and dignity of every human person created in the image and likeness of God. Let us admit to our lack of commitment to issues of justice and peace in the world and in our own communities.

All pray Lord, God of all peoples and every nation, you created the human race in your own image and likeness. You care for each of us and make no distinctions between us. We have not remained faithful to our calling to welcome, nurture and care for our brothers and sisters, especially those who cannot change their situations. We have practised discrimination and intolerance against those who are different. We lament the ways in which we have failed to promote, defend and share basic human rights with those who are of a different race or colour, age, intellectual or physical disability, gender or sexual orientation, faith or economic condition. For these sins we ask your pardon and merciful forgiveness.

Pause

Presider Accept our resolve as a Church to promote, defend and sustain the basic human rights and dignity of all persons, since each and every human being is a reflection of your divine image and is called to be the crowning splendour of your creation. We ask this through Jesus Christ, the one true shepherd, yesterday, today and forever.

Response Amen.

All sing Kyrie, Kyrie, Kyrie eleison

**VII Sin Against Children**

Reader Let us pray for young children who have suffered as a result of violence, sexual abuse and family trauma. Let us acknowledge how we may have failed at times to protect or safeguard their innocence. Let us seek forgiveness for any misconduct committed against children.

All pray God of all wonder and love, you give the human family the gift of children, who reflect to us the beauty of your infinite love. We lament the lack of compassion and sensitivity in responding to those who suffer as a result of any form of violence inflicted on them as children. For these sins we ask your pardon and merciful forgiveness.

Pause

Presider Accept our resolve as a Church to work always to protect our young people from any form of abuse – psychological, physical or sexual. We shall deepen our commitment to assist anyone who has been victimised and to bring them and their families the healing and compassion they need. We ask this, through Jesus Christ, the innocent victim, yesterday, today and forever.

Response Amen.

All sing Kyrie, Kyrie, Kyrie eleison

**VIII Sin Against the Unity of the Church**
Reader Let us pray for the unity of Christians, that we may realise what we can do together to spread Christ's message of peace and understanding. We remember also those who feel alienated from the Church, from their parish communities, and those who have left the faith.

All pray Gracious God, we acknowledge the scandal of division and animosity that at times exists between ourselves and our fellow Christians. We regret any contribution we have made to the feelings of estrangement that some experience within our Church and we are saddened by their pain. For these sins we ask your pardon and merciful forgiveness.

Pause

Presider Accept our resolve as a Church to work for the unity of Christians. May we realise the bonds between us and imitate in love and charity the One after whom we are called. May we also be people who offer healing to those who feel alienated from the Church at this time. We ask this through Jesus Christ, who prayed that we may all be one yesterday, today and forever.

Response Amen.

All sing Kyrie, Kyrie, Kyrie eleison

**Rite of Reconciliation**
All present could be invited to look at other areas of personal sinfulness in a spirit of quiet and reflection.

*Preparation for the Sacrament of Reconciliation*
This reflection might focus on three aspects of reconciliation – with each other, with the wider community and with God.

Lord, I am taken up with the many issues that may not affect me personally. Help me to see the divisions in my relationships with others in my life. Give me the courage to make the first step on the road to reconciliation.

A Thiarna, déan trócaire.

Lord, I try to convince myself that my sins don't affect other people. Open my eyes to the communal implications of my actions and lead me to the place of reconciliation.

A Chríost, déan trócaire.

Lord of gentleness and compassion, I know that I should not fear meeting you face to face in the Sacrament of Reconciliation. Help me in my anxiety and give me the humility to accept your healing grace.

A Thiarna, déan trócaire.

The Act of Sorrow is then recited. Individual Confession and Absolution may then follow while music is played or sung. Each person is invited to venerate the cross before Confession and is given a token such as the Cross in my Pocket wooden disc or a prayer card. Be mindful of those who may be upset by the issues covered in the service and allow discreet space for them to be supported.

*Music Suggestions at this time:*
*Crucem Tuam* (Taizé)
*Jesus The Lord* (Roc O'Connor)
*Behold The Wood* (Dan Schutte)
*All You Who Pass This Way* (Taizé)
*We Remember* (Marty Haugen – *Gather*)

*Blessing of Crosses*
The ceremony will conclude with the blessing of crosses. The significance of wearing a cross and chain or a lapel cross is not always appreciated in a spiritual context. A formal blessing of crosses could be preceded by some words on the depth of meaning of the practice, which transcends the merely cosmetic.

> May the Cross of Christ protect you from danger and harm.
> May the Cross of Christ guide you on the path of selfless love.
> May the Cross of Christ fill you with hope in moments of despair.

*Sign of Peace*
The Prayer of Saint Francis of Assisi, *Make Me A Channel Of Your Peace,* could then be sung by all and followed by the exchange of a sign of peace.

Sister Patricia Holden CHC and the Liturgy Group at All Hallows College, Drumcondra prepared an Advent Service of Reconciliation. This liturgy was based on *Service for the Healing of Memories* – Origins 15 November 2001, Vol. 31: No 23. *A Service of Lamentation – Recognising the Sins of our History.* Using this model, this liturgy was shaped for a celebration of reconciliation in Holy Week or around the cross on Good Friday.

# HOLY SATURDAY – MORNING PRAYER

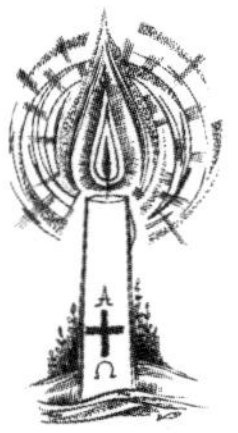

JOHN MCCANN

Today, the second day of the triduum, is a day of waiting, of continued meditation on the passion and death of Jesus, and on his descent to the dead. It is a day that is often missed or passed over in the movement from Good Friday to the vigil of Easter Sunday.

The meaning of today's liturgy is beautifully expressed in some of the texts of the Orthodox liturgy:

> He who holds the earth in the hollow of his hand is held fast by the earth; put to death according to the flesh, He delivers the dead from the grasping hand of hell.
>
> The life-giving Seed, twofold in nature, today is sown with tears in the furrows of the earth; but springing up He will bring joy to the world.
>
> When she received you in her bosom, O Creator and Saviour, the earth shook in fear, and with her quaking she awoke the dead.
>
> A stone hewn from the rock covers the Cornerstone; and a mortal man now buries God in the grave as one dead. Tremble, O earth!
>
> Hell was wounded in the heart when it received Him whose side was pierced by the spear; consumed by divine fire it groaned aloud at our salvation who sing, O God our Deliverer, blessed are You.

For the meaning of this day to come alive for people, some liturgical celebration is needed. Many people would be happy to spend some time in prayer on Holy Saturday morning. The celebration of the Office of Readings and Morning Prayer is strongly recommended today. Other liturgies of the word or devotions are also possible. The full texts of Morning Prayer are given in the Breviary. Where the use of the full text given there is not feasible for congregational participation, the simplified celebration below may be more helpful.

**Celebrating Morning Prayer**
The celebration of the Morning Prayer comes alive when the texts are sung. For this reason a number of different options are presented for each element, in the hope that a version which can be readily sung may be used. The pieces are such that only a cantor is needed to lead the congregation and to sing some verses.

The text of one psalm is given, together with its antiphon for the day. If desired, the psalm could be prayed responsorially, with the antiphon repeated by the congregation after each verse. It is, however, preferable to have a sung psalm.

Liturgical planners might wish to think of some visual focus that will help the prayer of the gathering. Examples would be: the cross, an image of the sorrowful Virgin Mary, or a representation of the tomb. A brief gesture of veneration of an image such as this is possible at the end of the service.

*Opening Verse*

All stand

Leader: O God, come to our aid.

All: O Lord, make haste to help us.
Glory be to the Father, and to the Son, and to the Holy Spirit,
As it was in the beginning, is now and ever shall be,
world without end. Amen.

*Hymn*
The cross still stands on calv'ry hill,
Tree of a new and blessed life;
And in a garden close at hand
The Lord of Life and Death lies still.

The peace of death enfolds him now,
Anguish and pain can do no more.
The Victor-Victim for our sins
He sleeps awhile to rise again.

To Christ who died for love of us,
Bearing our sins before the throne,
To Father and to Paraclete
Be glory till the end of time.*

Other possible hymns:
*Unless a Grain of Wheat* by Bernadette Farrell (*In Caelo, Celebration Hymnal*)
*O Loving Wisdom of our God* (given in the Breviary. Tune: *Praise to the Holiest* or *St Columba*)
*Be Still and Know That I Am God* (Anon. *Celebration Hymnal, Hymns Old and New*)

*Psalm*

*Antiphon*
They will mourn for him as for an only son, since it is the innocent one of the Lord who has been slain.

*Psalm 63 (64)*
Hear my voice, O God, as I complain,
guard my life from dread of the foe.
Hide me from the band of the wicked,
from the throng of those who do evil.

---

* This can be sung to the tune of *All People That On Earth Do Dwell*, or any other tune of a similar metre.

They sharpen their tongues like swords;
they aim bitter words like arrows
to shoot at the innocent from ambush,
shooting suddenly and recklessly.

They scheme their evil course;
they conspire to lay secret snares.
They say: 'Who will see us?
Who can search out our crimes?'

He will search who searches the mind
and knows the depths of the heart.
God has shot them with his arrow
and dealt them sudden wounds.
Their own tongue has brought them to ruin
and all who see them mock.

Then all the world will fear;
they will tell what God has done.
They will understand God's deeds.
The just will rejoice in the Lord
and fly to him for refuge.
All the upright hearts will glory.

Glory be to the Father, and to the Son, and to the Holy Spirit,
as it was in the beginning, is now and ever shall be,
world without end. Amen.

*Antiphon*
They will mourn for him as for an only son, since it is the innocent one of the Lord who has been slain.

Alternative Psalms
*May Your Love Be Upon Us O Lord* (Margaret Daly – *Alleluia Amen*)
*Out of the Depths* (Joseph Gelineau – *Alleluia Amen, Hosanna*)
*The Lord is My Light and My Help* (Paul Inwood – *Music for the Reception of the Body at the Church*)
*Bless the Lord My Soul* (Taizé – *Celebration Hymnal*)

*Scripture Reading*
Hosea 6:1-3a
Come, let us return to the Lord. He has torn us to pieces, but he will heal us; he has struck us down, but he will bandage our wounds; after a day or two he will bring us back to life, on the third day he will raise us and we shall live in his presence.

*Antiphon*
A sung antiphon may follow the reading, for example:

*Christ Was Humbler Yet* (A. Milner – *Veritas Hymnal*)
*Meditation on the Passion* (Chris Walker – *Music for the Mass I*)

*Gospel Canticle*
All stand and sing or recite the canticle.

Blessed be the Lord, the God of Israel!
He has visited his people and redeemed them.

He has raised up for us a mighty saviour
in the house of David his servant,
as he promised by the lips of holy men,
those who were his prophets from of old.

A saviour who would free us from our foes,
from the hands of all who hate us.
So his love for our fathers is fulfilled
and his holy covenant remembered.

He swore to Abraham our father to grant us,
that free from fear, and saved from the hands of our foes,
we might serve him in holiness and justice
all the days of our life in his presence.

As for you, little child,
you shall be called a prophet of God, the Most High.
You shall go ahead of the Lord
to prepare his ways before him,

To make known to his people their salvation
through forgiveness of all their sins,
the loving kindness of the heart of our God
who visits us like the dawn from on high.

He will give light to those in darkness,
those who dwell in the shadow of death,
and guide us into the way of peace.

Glory be to the Father, and to the Son, and to the Holy Spirit,
as it was in the beginning, is now and ever shall be,
world without end. Amen.

The following version of the canticle may be sung to a simple tune such as *St Columba* (the same tune as *The King of Love My Shepherd Is*) or *Amazing Grace:*

Now bless the God of Israel, who comes in love and pow'r,
Who raises from the royal house deliverance in this hour.

Through holy prophets God has sworn to free us from alarm,
To save us from the heavy hand of all who wish us harm.

Remembering the covenant, God rescues us from fear,
That we might serve in holiness and peace from year to year;

And you, my child, shall go before to preach, to prophesy,
that all may know the tender love, the grace of God most high.

In tender mercy, God will send the dayspring from on high,
Our rising sun, the light of life for those who sit and sigh.

God comes to guide our way to peace, that death shall reign no more.
Sing praises to the Holy One! O worship and adore!

Another version of the canticle, by Howard Hughes SM, is in *Seinn Alleluia 2000.*

*Intercessions*
Leader Let us pray to Christ, who suffered and died for us, was buried, and rose again from the dead. A Thiarna, déan trócaire.

All A Thiarna, déan trócaire.

(Some other sung response may be substituted.)

Reader Christ our Saviour, your Mother stood sorrowing at the cross and at the tomb: give us strength at those moments when we share in your sufferings. (R)

Reader Christ our Lord, like a grain of wheat falling to the ground, you gained for us a harvest of divine life: help us to die to sin and to live for God alone. (R)

Reader Good Shepherd, you remained in the tomb, hidden from mortal sight: teach us to love our life with you, which is hidden in God. (R)

Reader: Jesus, the new Adam, you descended to the realm of the dead that you might free the just from the fetters of death: may people everywhere hear the liberating sound of your voice, and be freed from sin. (R)

Reader: Christ, Son of the living God, we have been buried with you in Baptism: may we rise with you and walk in newness of life. (R)

The *Our Father* is recited or sung by all.

*Concluding Rite*

*Prayer*
It was you, Father, who watched over your Son,
and in you his body rested in safety.
The guard at his tomb knew only the fear of death;
but for the Virgin Mary
and those who watched with her,
you prepared the dawn of a new creation.
Forgive all those who still today imprison life.
Open the hearts of all to hope
in Jesus, your Son, our Lord.

All Amen.

As a final act of veneration, people might like to come forward individually and place flowers in front of the cross or another suitable image. Meanwhile one of the following could be sung:

*Jesus, Remember Me* (Taizé)
*I See His Blood Upon The Rose* (Michael Joncas – *Hosanna*)
*Tree of Life* (Marty Haugen – *Gather*)

# EASTER VIGIL
# SAMPLE WORDS OF INTRODUCTION

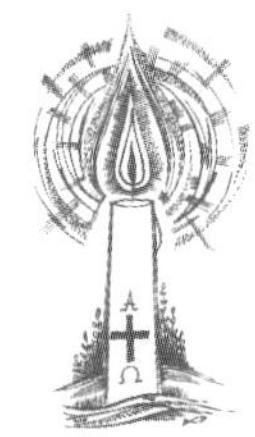

JOHN MCCANN

*Some words of introduction may be helpful before the celebration begins. If the weather is still cold, people sometimes tend to gather inside the church instead of outside (although a really big paschal fire will provide warmth!). Words of introduction a few moments before the beginning of the liturgy can also include an invitation to go outside.*

Good evening, and welcome to our celebration of the Easter Vigil.

The foundation of tonight's celebration is the Liturgy of the Word, in which we retell the stories of God who saves his people, creating light in the darkness, bringing freedom to those enslaved, bringing hope to the faint-hearted, bringing new life out of death. This is the story of our lives too. We can enter more deeply into the celebration by listening to God speaking to us through the scriptures and by singing the responses, so that God's word may enter more deeply into our hearts.

One of the highlights of tonight's celebration is the moment when we welcome N.____________ as a new member of the Christian community. It is a moment for us to renew our own baptismal promises also and to be sprinkled with the same water with which N.______________ is baptised.

The climax of our vigil, and indeed the culmination of our three days of prayer and celebration, is the moment when the Lord Jesus gathers us around the table of the Eucharist, inviting us to taste and see the goodness of his life, poured out for us. The meaning of this liturgy is so profound that we will continue to celebrate it for the next fifty days.

But first we will begin tonight's celebration with the ancient Irish custom of lighting a fire in honour of Jesus, the light of the world. Then the paschal candle is prepared. It is decorated with five grains of incense in memory of the wounds of Christ who died for us. The candle is then lit and carried in procession into the church; just as the people of Israel were led by a pillar of fire on their Exodus journey from slavery to freedom, so, too, we follow the light of Christ, knowing that we do not walk in darkness. Then we listen to the *Exsultet*, the great song of praise and thanksgiving in honour of Christ, who broke the chains of death and rose triumphant from the grave.

Before we begin, you are encouraged to make your way outside to take part in this dramatic opening to our celebration.

# CELEBRATING THE EASTER VIGIL

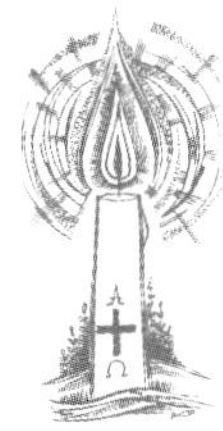

JULIE KAVANAGH

**Some Preliminary Remarks**

- The celebration of the Easter Vigil is part of our overall celebration of the Easter Triduum. These three days represent one moment of celebration, i.e. we are greeted at the beginning of the Thursday Evening Mass and are not dismissed again until the end of the Easter Vigil on Holy Saturday.

- Therefore, when we are making our preparations to celebrate the Easter Vigil, we need to do so with a definite eye to how we are going to celebrate the other liturgies of the triduum.

- Unique rituals, such as those of the triduum, can be fully effective only if they are substantially the same from year to year – so that people can enter into them with confidence.

- If we keep a good record of what is done each year, we are in a position to build on and enhance the tradition of celebration in the parish. So keep notes and evaluate the liturgies with the parish liturgy group as soon as possible after the triduum. Recommendations can then be made and followed through at next year's parish celebration of the triduum.

- Liturgy is made up of many elements, including community, Word, action, environment, movement, gestures, postures, processions, senses (smell, touch, hearing, sight…), symbols, ministries, music… Think of all these elements when making your preparations.

- If we allow these days to speak for themselves and to have their full effect on us, we will inevitably be changed, renewed and reoriented on the Christian journey.

**The Easter Vigil – a Journey of Four Stages**

The Easter Vigil is made up of four stages:

The Service of Light
The Liturgy of the Word
The Liturgy of Baptism
The Liturgy of the Eucharist

In preparing this night's liturgy the following questions and ideas might be helpful:

*The Service of Light*

As an introductory rite, the Service of Light gathers and readies us as one community to hear the Word of God. It begins by the Easter fire and concludes with the singing of the *Exsultet.*

- At what time will the Service of Light begin? It is presumed that the vigil will take place in darkness. The Met Office can provide you with the time of sunset and you can plan accordingly. Remember that this is the first celebration of Easter Sunday and should not be anticipated by any other parish Mass!

- Where will the Easter fire be located? Ideally it should be located outside so that priests, ministers and at least some of the community can gather around it. If some of the assembly remain in the church for this part of the liturgy, explore ways in which they might hear what is taking place, taking into account the sound system in your particular location. *(Given the Irish climate, it is always wise to have a plan B – perhaps a contained fire at the back of the church. But have the desired intention to opt for an outside fire.)*

- Where will the Easter candle be brought to at the end of the opening procession? The Easter candle can be left either by the baptistry or in close proximity to the ambo. If we choose to place the candle by the ambo we are giving ourselves a visible reminder that the readings we proclaim this night, and in all our liturgies, make sense to us through the eyes of Easter faith. The candle can be kept in place by the ambo until the end of the Easter season.

- Who will we need for this stage of the liturgy? The local scouts or guides or other youth group could be enlisted to build the fire outside. Ushers will be needed to guide people when the church is in darkness and to help guide the procession into the church. Ushers might also ensure that everyone present has a candle that will be lit from the Easter candle and a participation sheet. A cantor or cantors will be needed to proclaim in song the *Exsultet*, if a deacon is not doing so. A group might be invited to prepare the space in the church where the Easter candle is to be left, i.e. a garland of flowers might be in place at the base of the candle-stand. Altar servers will be needed at this part of the vigil, as throughout.

- When should the candles held by the people be extinguished? From a practical point of view it may make sense to extinguish these candles after the singing of the *Exsultet.* Rather than give a long instruction, people can be encouraged to extinguish their candles through the example of those in the sanctuary area. If the presider and other ministers simply, and with some style and grace(!), blow out their candles, the people will follow in their action.

- What music will be used at this stage? After the lighting of the Easter candle there follow three sung acclamations, which are staggered during the procession from the fire to the sanctuary area. These acclamations are found in the *Sacramentary.* There are a number of sung versions of the *Exsultet* outside of the one provided in the *Sacramentary.* Some of these are very assembly friendly and are worth exploring.

- Choreography In preparing this stage of the liturgy, think out how the actions of processions, lighting candles, etc. will be choreographed.

- Incense For the opening procession, have a thurible ready to be lit from the Easter fire. Remember that as the *Exsultet* is sung, the Easter candle is incensed. What kind of incense does the parish use? – is it hypo-allergenic? What does it conjure up on our sense of smell?

**Preparatory Rites**

- Decide ahead of time whether you are going to do the preparatory rites for the candle, as these are optional.

- The Easter candle itself Perhaps this would be an appropriate year to evaluate the quality of the Easter candle used in the parish. Is it of good crafting and quality? If not, is this the year to explore an alternative make of candle that is worthy of its role as the Easter candle?

*The Liturgy of the Word*
The lighting of the Easter candle and the hymn of praise sung in the *Exsultet* brings us to a point where we are ready to hear our story. It is the telling of our story that is at the heart of the vigil. In the light of Easter faith, in the light of the Easter candle, we allow ourselves a time of waiting and listening. In the stories of creation, liberation and rebirth we hear not 'history' but 'our story'.

- How many readings will be proclaimed on the night? In the Roman liturgy we are provided with nine readings – seven from the Old Testament and two from the New Testament (the Epistle and the Gospel). For pastoral reasons the number of Old Testament readings can be reduced to as little as two, with Exodus 14 never being omitted. However, given that the Word of God is at the heart of our vigil, we should aim to give people a real experience of waiting and listening.

- Choreography Again when preparing this Liturgy of the Word think of its choreography. It is possible to thread a Liturgy of the Word together that consists of the different components of Word, action, movement, music, song and silence. When doing so we should think of the pace and movement of the Word so as not to overburden any one reading with all the elements of creativity to the detriment of the proclamation of another reading.

- Who will we need to minister during this part of the liturgy? Given the centrality of this celebration in our Church year, this is not an occasion to have one lector proclaim all the readings! (Ideally, of course, this should never be the case!) Tonight's Liturgy of the Word should reflect a sense of the importance of the Word of God in our lives by its vibrancy and the obvious care and effort that has gone into its preparation. We can be creative in how we communicate the Word of God through the use of musicians, our best lectors, some ministers of movement/gesture and the gift of silence.

- The Gloria With the singing of the *Gloria* we welcome back the church bells that have fallen silent since the *Gloria* of the Holy Thursday evening liturgy. As well as ringing its church bells during this hymn, a parish might decide to invite parishioners to bring their own small bells to be rung during the refrain of the *Gloria.* This is an element of the liturgy that can be built upon in years to come so that families will bring them on Holy Thursday, Holy Saturday and for Christmas day. As a start this year, a parish might decide to have the altar servers or some youth of the parish hold hand-held bells and ring them.

- Environment The *Gloria* marks the transition from the Old Testament to the New Testament in the Liturgy of the Word. It does so through the ringing of the church bells but also through the invitation to light the altar candles and the practice of decorating the altar with flowers. Some parishes have chosen to invite children to place flowers around the sanctuary area at this time. In practice, what this means is having pots of spring flowers, i.e. lily's, chrysanthemums, tulips, at the back of the church. Adults need to be in place both at the back and the front of the church to direct the children in the placing of the plants at this time. Some parishes have an Easter garden which could be added to/completed during the singing of the *Gloria.*

- The Alleluia It might be fair to say that it is not easy to appreciate fully the return of the *Alleluia* when it is only separated from the *Gloria* by an opening prayer and a reading. Without doubt the use of a real Gospel procession helps to build this appreciation. If a book of the Gospels is used it could be carried aloft through the body of people, with incense and the accompanying use of Psalm 117, with an *Alleluia* refrain. Putting the church lights on full might also emphasise the importance of the Gospel proclamation. In the *Alleluia* we should sense – see, hear and smell – the joy, colour, life and light of the Easter story.

- The Homily The presider might choose to offer a personal profession of Easter faith.

- Music There are a variety of options for music in this part of the Easter Vigil. The priorities for music are the *Alleluia* and the *Gloria.* The Liturgy of the Word does, of course, include the use of psalms. Some possibilities include using the set psalm for each reading; using the same psalm refrain throughout with a different verse after each reading.

*The Liturgy of Baptism*
In the light of the Easter candle we have shared our story until we triumphantly and joyfully proclaimed the emptiness of the tomb and the truth of the Resurrection. Because we have done this we can now go forward and do what we have really come to do – to baptise and share in the Eucharist.

- The Font It is essential that the font be seen by all present. If this is not the case, a large vessel of water may be placed in the sanctuary. Easter lilies can be placed around the font, together with the holy oils, white garment(s) and candles.

- The Litany of the Saints The litany of the saints accompanies the procession to the font. Names of local or patron saints can be added to the litany as appropriate. The procession consists of the Easter candle, candidates for Baptism together with their Godparents. (If children, rather than adults, are to be baptised, their parents also accompany them.) The people stand during this litany – a sign of their support and solidarity with those about to become members of the community.

- Blessing of the Water This beautiful prayer should be proclaimed solemnly with care. The Easter candle should be immersed in the water at the appropriate stage of the prayer. Suitable instrumental music might be played during the proclamation of this blessing prayer.

- Lighting of People's Candles The people's candles are lit for the renewal of their baptismal promises, which is done after the Baptism and its explanatory rites. The light from the Easter candle is passed to the assembly once the newly baptised have received their lighted candle, after the chrismation and the giving of the white garment. (If an adult is being fully initiated at the vigil, the people's renewal of baptismal promises takes place after the adult's confirmation.) A degree of patience is needed here – to wait until all the people have their candles lit before moving into the renewal of promises. This can be accelerated by having ushers primed to bring candles lit from the Easter candle to different corners of the church.

- Welcome Hopefully the newly baptised and their families will sense our welcome of them into our community. A warm applause at the end of the Baptism before the people's renewal of baptismal promises might be one way of communicating this welcome.

- Sprinkling Rite Of all the sprinkling rites of the year this is the one we really need to know how to celebrate! We are professing our faith in the joy of resurrection which we share through the waters of Baptism. How are we going to enable people to connect with this living water? If the presider is to sprinkle the people, what path will he take around the church? How will he reach as many people as possible with the water? Will people be able to see and feel this living water sailing through the air? Some parishes, in light of the size of their font and the design of their church, actually invite the people 'to come to the water'. To the accompaniment of song, the people come to the baptism font and generously bless themselves with this holy water.

- The General Intercessions On this night the newly baptised take part in these prayers for the first time. Even if we have not baptised in our own church, we remember now the thousands of people throughout the world who have joined our community tonight.

- Sample Introduction to the General Intercessions Dear friends in Christ, on this Easter night the whole world resounds in joy with the good news of resurrection. Filled with renewed strength and courage, we turn to our God in prayer – for our needs and the needs of all the world.

- Conclusion to the General Intercessions Creator God, in this time you renew us with the sacraments of your love. Fill us with the power flowing from Christ's Resurrection, that we may bring the meaning of the Resurrection to our live and the lives of all we meet.

- Music Sung music should accompany the procession to the font (the litany of the saints) and the sprinkling rite. A sung response to the general intercessions can underscore the festivity of this night. A joyful *Alleluia* could also be sung after Baptism has taken place.

*The Liturgy of the Eucharist*
It is through the celebration of the Eucharist that the Church continues to celebrate the Resurrection of the Lord. Therefore, although the rite remains unchanged in relation to the Sunday celebration, we should avoid the temptation to rush this element of the night.

- Who prepares the altar? If Baptism has taken place, it is fitting that the newly baptised – or their parents in the case of children – bring the bread and wine to the table of God. Other members of the community can be invited to dress the altar with a large white cloth, corporal and flowers to add to the festivity of this night. It might make more sense to light the candles around the altar at this point rather than at the *Gloria.*

- Gifts of Bread and Wine This might be a perfect opportunity to reflect on the bread we use for our liturgies in our community. Does it look and taste like bread, as is called for? Might we think about using larger, more substantial bread, like that produced by the Glencairn community? We might also pause to reflect on the vessels we use. Are our chalices and ciboria of good quality and well-crafted?

- Take and Eat, Take and Drink Tonight we might also seek to answer the call of Jesus to take and eat, take and drink. Could we invite people to share in the cup this night? If so, what practical things do we need to do in order to prepare for this?

- Eucharistic Prayer Ahead of this year's celebration of the Easter Vigil we might reflect on our posture as a community during this prayer. Are we consistent, clear and unified on when and why we kneel/sit/stand? To highlight the centrality of this prayer, if the presider is gifted with a musical voice, would it be possible to use one of the sung settings of this prayer?

- Music The acclamations of the Eucharistic Prayer should share a common setting to express their unity. Is there a setting of the Lord's Prayer that could be sung as a community? The Ó

Riada and Estelle White settings are very familiar to people. The song accompanying the communion procession should invite the people to participate while processing. Therefore, it is helpful to use a hymn with an easily remembered refrain. Examples include *To Be Your Bread* – David Haas; *Eat this Bread* – Jacques Berthier; *Table of Plenty* – Dan Schutte; *I Will be the Vine* – Liam Lawton; *I am the Bread of Life* – Suzanne Toolan; *Jesus Christ Yesterday, Today and Forever* – Suzanne Toolan. For the closing song it is hard to beat *Jesus Christ is Risen Today,* while there are certainly others from which to choose, including *All Creatures of Our God and King.*

- Sending Forth At the end of this night, parishes might arrange to have a cup of tea for people, if there is a parish hall available to them. If this is possible, why not bless an Easter cake after communion that will be shared with those who stay for the cuppa. Alternatively, parents might bring Easter eggs for their children, which could be blessed before the final dismissal. This after-vigil social is a good way to continue the welcome of new members to the community.

- Don't forget to sing the double *Alleluia* of the dismissal, which continues throughout the Easter season.

- Finally, don't worry if you feel exhausted at the end of this liturgy – you will be in a good position to appreciate truly the joy and renewal of resurrection!

# MUSIC RESOURCES – THE EASTER VIGIL

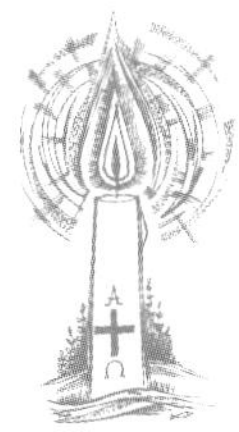

PAT O'DONOGHUE

**Service of Light**
For weeks before Hallowe'en young people can be seen gathering the ingredients for their bonfire. Why not harness this spirit and youthful energy in the preparation of materials for the Easter fire. Let the fire in its glory be a real beacon in the community. Before the liturgy begins, music could be played around the fire and people encouraged to gather, to listen or to move to what they hear. Invite local traditional musicians to be part of this through the local branch of Comhaltas Ceoltóirí Éireann. Jugglers with fire might also enhance the spirit of the evening. The length of the vigil ceremony and its many layers can be offputting for some. Consider inviting people to meet around the fire and for the Ceremony of Light. Some will follow into the church for the *Exsultet: the Easter Proclamation.* Some might drift off home or to other social events, while others will leave after the singing of the Easter Proclamation. Perhaps they will keep vigil in their own way.

During the Blessing of the Candle the music group might sing the setting from the Monks of Weston Priory – *Christ Yesterday and Today.* The Procession to the Church could be accompanied by *The Lord is My Light* (Taizé), which would be stopped at each stage to allow for the singing of the traditional *Light of Christ/Lumen Christi.* There are several versions of the *Exsultet.* You might consider Margaret Daly Denton's setting published by Veritas and also available on tape.

**Liturgy of the Word**
The Responsorial Psalms during this part of the vigil can help to build the atmosphere of waiting, celebration and rejoicing. A variety of settings and suggestions are given below:

1. Psalm 103
*Send Forth Your Spirit* (*Psalms for Holy Week* – Irish Institute for Pastoral Liturgy)
*Lord Send Out Your Spirit* (Paul Lisicky – *Gather*)

2. Psalm 15
*Preserve Me, God, I Take Refuge In You* (Dal McNulty – *Alleluia Amen*)
*For You Are My God* (St Louis Jesuits – NALR)

3. Song of Moses – Exodus 15:1-6,17-18
*I Will Sing to the Lord* (Stephen Dean – *The Great Week*, McCrimmon Publishing Co.)
*Song of Moses* (Betty Ann Pulkingham – *Gather*)

4. Psalm 29
*I Will Praise You Lord* (Laurence Bevenot – *The Great Week*)
*I Will Praise You Lord* (*Psalms for Holy Week – IIPL*)

5. Isaiah 12:2-6
*We Shall Draw Water Joyfully* (Paul Inwood – *The Great Week*)
*With Joy You Will Draw Water* (Ian Forrester – *The Great Week*)

6. Psalm 18
*Lord You Have The Words* (Marty Haugen – *Psalms for the Church Year,* Vol. 1)
*You Have The Message Of Eternal Life* (*Psalms for Holy Week* – IIPL)

7. Psalms 41 and 42
*Like The Deer That Yearns* (Joseph Walshe – *Alleluia Amen*)
*Like The Deer That Yearns* (Tony Barr – *The Great Week*)

8. Alleluia – Psalm 117
*Alleluia* (Fintan O'Carroll and Chris Walker – *The Great Week*)
*Alleluia* (*Psalms for Holy Week* – IIPL)

**Liturgy of Baptism**
A musical link throughout this part of the rite could be useful. The refrain of *We Shall Draw Water Joyfully* would suit this purpose. It could be used as the acclamation when the candle is taken out of the water and during the sprinkling of the people. The Plainsong *Vidi Aquam* is also particularly apt at this latter point.

**Mass Settings**
The singing of the *Gloria* is particularly special on this night. Opinions vary on the use of the large Polyphonic or Classic Mass settings or the alternative use of modern settings with a refrain for the congregation. The local liturgy group will know what will best suit their situation. The setting of the Eucharistic Prayer Acclamations should have the possibility of full involvement either by familiarity or by easy access through a responsorial style. *The Mass of Our Lady of Lourdes* inspires the use of trumpets and has unity of style (albeit by different composers) which enhances that important element of the Eucharistic Prayer. Richard Proulx's *Community Mass* allows for repetition of the acclamations with participation in view and with further enhancement of the choir's role. *The Glastonbury Mass* by Chris Walker is completely responsorial and can be sung by all, even if never heard before. John McCann's *Let Me Hear Your Voice* setting is also congregation-friendly. Marty Haugen's *Mass of Creation* lends itself very well to participation by the frequent use of a motif. You may have your own particular settings and, once again, the local liturgy group will make this important choice.

Relax in the memory of 'Those Three Days' which you have helped to celebrate. Keep in mind, however, that this is only the beginning of the Easter celebrations – there are fifty more days to go.

# EASTER VIGIL – SACRISTAN'S LIST

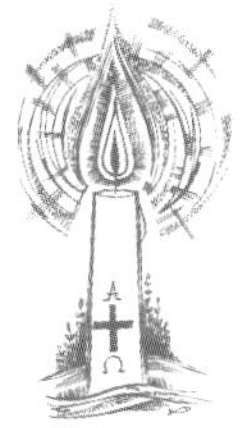

JOHN MCCANN

**Sacristy**

- White Mass vestments
- Candles [with paper holders] for priests and servers
- Thurible (prepared with lighting charcoal) and boat
- Paschal candle:
  - Wick tipped with methylated spirits for easy lighting
  - A transparent plastic shield around the top of the candle to protect the flame from the wind (should be easily removable)
  - Holes prepared in the candle for insertion of the grains of incense
- A pocket torch
- *Roman Missal*

**Outside the Church**

- Microphone if needed [tested]
- Paschal fire
- Table covered with a white cloth:
  - Stylus for incising the candle
  - Five grains of incense on a salver
  - Taper (if necessary tied to a long stick, to prevent it dropping in the heat of the fire)

If wet weather threatens, a smaller-scale fire may be needed in a covered area.

**Sanctuary**

- Stand for the paschal candle

**The Place of Baptism**

Hopefully a Baptism will be taking place. This normally takes place at the baptismal font. If the font cannot be seen by the congregation, a large container of water is used in the sanctuary itself for the Baptism. This could be suitably decorated with flowers. In some churches it will be possible to have all of this in place before the liturgy begins; in other locations, it may be necessary for items to be carried into position at the time of Baptism. If necessary, a microphone may be used at this place.

Nearby

- a jug
- a towel
- chrism
- cotton wool
- empty holy water container and sprinkler

- baptismal candle
- the *Rite of Baptism for Chidren* or the *Rite of Christian Initiation of Adults*, depending on whether children or adults are to be baptised.

Altar
- cloth, corporal
- microphone behind
- The altar candles are in place but not lit. (The wicks can be prepared with methylated spirits for easy lighting.)
- The cross is in its usual place.
- The Book of Gospels may be on the altar.

**Ambo**
- Lectionary, marked for the Easter Vigil

**Credence Table**
- Two candlesticks, unlighted, for use in the final procession
- Tapers
- Bowl and towel
- Chalice(s) as needed
- Purificator(s)

**Table of Gifts**
- Bread and wine, as needed for all who will receive

# REFLECTIONS ON THE OLD TESTAMENT READINGS OF THE EASTER VIGIL

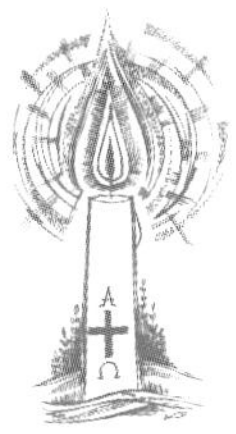

JOHN McCANN

The Liturgy of the Word is the foundation on which the Easter Vigil is built, and yet we know it can be difficult for people to follow and to understand. The Old Testament readings in particular present a challenge. The full sequence of readings is long, and yet vigils are, by their very nature, lengthy. Over the centuries the number of readings in the Roman rite has varied from four to twelve.

To a certain extent one needs to be familiar with the readings if one is really to hear them and appreciate them. I believe that one of the keys to liturgical renewal is, paradoxically, more private reading of scripture. We need to learn through personal meditation to love the wisdom and inspiration that these great texts give us. We need to discover in a truly personal way that the scriptures can really become the springboard for a conversation with God. What I suggest in this chapter is that the vigil readings could be used for meditation and reflection in the days and weeks that lead up to the vigil. This could be done on one's own or in a group. The readings could in fact become the basis of a whole Lenten programme. Those who will proclaim the readings would benefit particularly from this kind of remote preparation.

There are some brief notes on each reading that may be of help. They make particular reference to the fact that the readings will be proclaimed and heard during the Easter Vigil, in the context of Baptism into the death and resurrection of Christ. Some reflective questions follow – these might lead quite naturally into a prayer conversation. Simple activities are also suggested as ways of digesting the ideas or images. Other activities may also suggest themselves – to read the text out loud or to write it out longhand are, for example, traditional methods used to apply oneself more fully to the text.

**The First Reading**
This reading is a solemn proclamation of God the Creator. The majestic rhythm of the text insists repeatedly on the transforming power of God's word: 'God said… and it was so'. God's delight in creation also recurs like a refrain: 'And God saw that it was good'.

Despite this great affirmation of faith, we know that not all is right in the world. Our world is disfigured by violence and selfishness. The coming of Christ among us is, therefore, the beginning of the 'remaking' of our world. This process is irreversible. The one who created light out of darkness is the same one who raised Jesus from the dead. Evil will not have the last word. We are invited to become part of the new creation. The healing of our world begins in my own heart: I must be changed by God's love, transformed, refashioned into the image of God that I am intended to be.

**Questions for Reflection**

1. The spirit of God hovered over the dark, chaotic waters in the formless void. What are the 'dark places' in my life? Are these in fact the places where God's spirit can begin to re-create?
2. We are stewards of creation. What is my attitude to the environment? Am I caring in my use of the good things of creation?

**Actions**

1. Take some time to linger with the different good things that God has created. Watch the dawn. Visit the seaside, lake or river. Look out for the moon and stars. Enjoy animals – even the local cats or dogs!
2. Think of a famous saint whom you admire and find out more about her/him. In what way is (s)he an image of God?

**Prayer**

By your word, O Lord,
the heavens were made,
the stars, the oceans and the seas.
Open our eyes to appreciate the
even greater wonders you wish to work
in the heart of each of us.

**Second Reading**

The story of the sacrifice of Abraham seems intolerable to some. It seems inconceivable that God would, even as a test, ask someone to be ready to kill their child. Yet we know that human sacrifices were common in the ancient world. The outcome of the story is, however, that human sacrifice is not the way. Perhaps this story was first written to teach quite clearly that God does not want human sacrifice. The story also gives us a graphic picture of Abraham's extraordinary faith in the face of the threat of terrible loss. In the Easter Triduum we consider with awe the fact that God endured what Abraham was spared: God gave up his Son, his only Son. In the Genesis story the life of Isaac was spared; he went to the brink of the grave and came back. Jesus, the Son of God, went beyond the brink: he was buried in the tomb and came back victorious. Each Easter, countless numbers of adults enter into the death and resurrection of Jesus through Baptism and become descendants of Abraham through faith.

**Questions for Reflection**

1. This story is shot through with images of death and life. Have there been times in my life when I thought that something was dying within me, only to discover later that it was the beginning of new life? What are the 'sorrowful mysteries' of my life? Did any of them ever usher in unexpected newness of life?
2. What does God want me to do with my time and talents? What do I want God to provide for me?
3. Is there anything dying within me at the moment? What is it like?

**Actions**

1. Visit the graves of family or relations.
2. Buy some seeds or bulbs. Bury them in the earth and wait for them to grow.

**Prayer**

You call us, Lord Jesus, to follow you
along the path of life and death.

Attune our hearts to the music of your voice,
and teach us to trust your promptings,
that we may experience happiness with you for ever.

**Third Reading**

The crossing of the sea by the Israelites is not just a geographical journey. A providential escape by means of wind and tide has grown into a great story of epic proportions, a story that is ours too. It is a journey from slavery to freedom. It is a journey of discovering a God who saves and liberates. A journey made safe by God, who holds back the threat of drowning and death. In his great exodus journey, Jesus himself has passed from this world to the Father, opening the way for us to follow. Our willingness to be drenched with the waters of Baptism is a courageous undertaking to follow him as a people.

**Questions for Reflection**

1. The book of Exodus recounts how the Israelites were oppressed and burdened by Pharaoh. Where is the 'Pharaoh figure' in my heart? What enslaves me?
2. What are the burdens that oppress people today? In my family? In the area in which I live? In the world?
3. Moses is presented in the book of Exodus as a timid and reluctant leader and yet his role was essential. In what way am I called to be like Moses, to take charge of things, to bring relief to myself or others?
4. The Israelites crossed over through the sea. What 'crossing' am I making at the moment? What 'crossing' is my parish community called to make in these days?

**Actions**

1. Find out your date and place of Baptism. Write it in your diary. Visit your place of Baptism if possible.
2. Take a large sheet of paper and draw on it your life's journey so far (cellotape some pages together if necessary). When were the 'epic moments'?
3. Give some donations to a charity committed to bringing relief to the oppressed.

**Prayer**

God our Saviour,
your Son passed through death into eternal life.
Amid the troubles and difficulties of life's journey,
keep us close to him whose love will always triumph:
Jesus, our risen Lord,
for ever and ever.

**Fourth Reading**

The pain of marriage breakdown is not far from many of us. An increasing number of couples suffer in this way. There are times when the demise of a relationship seems irreversible. Such was the feeling for the people of God in their time of exile in Babylon: they seemed to have been abandoned by God. But, for God, no breakdown is final. God's love always allows for a new beginning. Our relationship with God can always be rebuilt. The marriage image is a powerful way of describing how God wants to relate to us. It may seem too intimate a way of being with God, and yet this image has been part of Christian spirituality for centuries. The Letter to the Ephesians describes the Church as a Bride (Eph 5:25-28). Again it may be difficult for us to conceive that the Church, with all the imperfections and failures in Church life, could be so closely bound to Christ. God's promise is that no matter how God-forsaken or shaken our 'marriage' relationship seems, it can always be rebuilt.

**Questions for Reflection**

1. What are the words in this reading that describe the experience of the people? Are there times when I have felt like this? Does this description match in any way the experience of the Church?
2. What are the words in this reading that describe the attitude of God to the people? How do I apply them to myself and the Church today?
3. Is there any line in the reading that I could use as a 'motto' by which to live?

**Actions**

1. Think of some relationship in your own life that is perhaps neglected or shaken. Reach out through a phone call, card, gift or some other sign of appreciation.
2. Find out more about Christians of other denominations in your area. Where do they worship? Find out if you can attend one of their services and thus contribute in a small way to the healing of ecumenical relations.

**Prayer**

Jesus our redeemer,
with unshakeable love you took pity on us
and in your blood you sealed a new and everlasting covenant.
Bind us closely to you
and restore within us all that is broken or in need of healing.

**Fifth Reading**

This reading is crammed with life-giving images: water for the thirsty, corn, wine and milk, bread and rich food, lifc-giving rains that provide growth and food from the earth. All this is promised to those who will listen to God's word and respond by seeking the Lord and calling out to him. It expresses the joy and nourishment of our faith, which draws its life from God's word. At the Easter Vigil the image of life-giving water (which is taken up also in the psalm that follows) will have extra resonances for those who are to be baptised, as well as those who will renew their baptismal faith.

**Questions for Reflection**

1. Name five times recently when you felt truly nourished and satisfied in spirit. Did these moments have anything in common?
2. Name five times recently when you expended energy or resources on something that, in the end, failed to satisfy. Did these moments have anything in common?
3. The reading encourages us to 'seek the Lord'. How might I go about doing this?

**Actions**

1. Undertake a simple programme of daily Bible reading. If necessary, get advice on how to do this.
2. Next time you use holy water (for example, on entering a church), do it with gusto and enjoy it!

**Prayer**

O God, our strength and our song,
draw us to yourself
that our hearts may be nourished
and our longings satisfied.
Teach us to drink deeply from the wellspring of your love
in the heart of Christ.
Amen.

**Sixth Reading**

The search for human happiness and fulfilment is constant, and 'the key to happiness' is much sought after. Another name for 'the secret of happiness' might be 'wisdom' – the wisdom that understands the way things are and how life is best lived. We believe that the key to wisdom is to ask the question: 'What are God's ways?' It is God's own wisdom that brought this world into being. God's wisdom will teach us the path to walk in life, giving us light, peace and understanding. God's wisdom, the reading tells us, is especially revealed in the scriptures themselves. Wisdom is so highly prized that it is personified; she is the one who gives life and light to all who are faithful to her. The personification of wisdom is, of course, a literary device, but the followers of Jesus believe that in him God's wisdom has truly become visible. Jesus himself is, in a sense, God's wisdom in person. He is the one through whom all things were made; he is the light of the world; he is one who in his own living perfects and fulfils all that is to be found in the Old Testament scriptures. Above all, the death and resurrection of Jesus confound human wisdom and challenge us deeply about our scale of values. The life of those baptised into Christ is lived according to a surprising interpretation of what it means to be fully alive and fully human.

**Questions for Reflection**

1. Think of a person who strikes you as particularly wise. What is it about them that impresses you most?
2. Read the 'Sermon on the Mount' (Mt 5:1-7,29). Which of the sayings of Jesus given there strikes you as most challenging? Can you think of any ways in which Jesus in particular lived them out himself?
3. Have there been moments in my life when I 'forsook the fountain of wisdom'? What did it feel like?

**Action**

The following exercise in wisdom takes a week to complete. At the end of each day, take a moment or two to relive all that has happened during the day. Ask yourself the following question: what were the happiest moments of my day? Write down the answer. At the end of the week review your seven answers and ask God for the wisdom to discern what it is that makes for true happiness.

**Prayer**

God our Creator,
whose word gives fresh insight to our minds
and joy to our hearts,
help us to live more and more
according to the mind of Christ your Son,
who is Lord for ever and ever.

**Seventh Reading**

In the sixth century BC Jerusalem was invaded by Babylonians and the people were carried off into exile. In this reading we see Ezekiel breathing fresh hope into the lives of those devastated by the exile: God promises the restoration of their land and nation. But the renewal promised by God is not just about a return home and the control of land; it is above all a renewal of the heart. God will cleanse the hearts of his people and put his spirit in them, making them capable of remaining faithful to him. Those who are baptised are also purified, washed clean, and gifted with the Holy Spirit of God. This 'internal renewal' is something to be entered into again and again each Lent, and celebrated at the Easter Vigil.

**Questions for Reflection**

1. All the good things we have in life come from God; but they can turn into idols. What are the idols in my life?
2. Count the number of times the personal pronoun 'I' appears in the reading. What does that tell you about the dynamic of the spiritual life?

**Actions**

1. Search through the newspapers of the coming week, looking out for reports of people who have been exiled from their homeland.
2. Get in touch with the meaning of the word 'cleansing' (wash the windows or do some other form of 'spring cleaning'). Do it in a prayerful, meditative way.
3. Decide a time for celebrating the Sacrament of Reconciliation and prepare yourself well, perhaps drawing on some of the insights that these readings have given you.

**Prayer**

Breathe new life into your people, Lord, and guide us gently but surely in the amazing ways of your love. We ask this through Christ our Lord.

# HOW TO BUILD AN EASTER GARDEN IN YOUR CHURCH

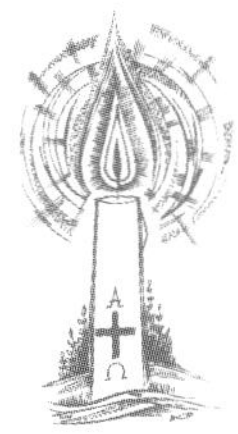

MARY HYNES

At the start of Lent, a garden is built in our church (St Gabriel's, Dollymount, Dublin) – a barren, desolate, desert area containing just sand and rocks with bare trees (large branches). The Easter garden follows on from the Lenten garden. The main features of the Easter garden are the tomb with the large boulder, flowing water, and plants (colourful flowers and leafy plants).

**The Tomb**

For the Easter Vigil the large boulder (made from sheets of polystyrene, plastered together) is moved from the entrance (made of polyzote). The inside of the tomb can be made to look like a cave by using heavy-duty black paper (available in four-foot sheets from Evans Mary's Abbey, Dublin). Concealed ultraviolet florescent tube lighting will pick out the white garments left lying about the tomb.

**The Water**

The waterfall is about four feet high. It consists of a fairly large immersion pump (with adjustable valves for altering the flow of water), a square base made from four wooden sleepers, with butryl sheeting stapled to the sides (this makes the base watertight). A wooden frame is made from marine ply, with all the joints sealed off with water-resistant glue. This allows the water to be piped up from the base and to flow from the top shelf of the frame, to create a waterfall effect. Stone, logs and rocks are placed around the sides of the base to give it a natural outdoor look.

**Flowers and Plants**

Each year we appeal to parishioners to help us with plants for the Easter garden. We ask them to lend or give us indoor flowering and green leafy plants – nothing precious or delicate. The response to these appeals has always been very generous. We look after the plants as well as we can and when we are dismantling the garden at the end of the season we gladly return all remaining plants to the owners.

For Easter Sunday we try to get as many daffodils as possible and these we put in oases in trays on tiered shelving, and in buckets, so as to provide as great a splash of colour as possible. The large wooden cross is placed in the garden in front of the tomb, free-standing on its side, with the crown of thorns laid on it.

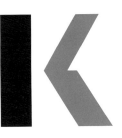

Kaplan Publishing are constantly finding new
ways to make a difference to you
exciting online resources really d
different to students looking for



This book comes with free MyKaplan online resources so that you can study anytime, anywhere. This free online resource is not sold separately and is included in the price of the book.

Having purchased this book, you have access to the following online study materials:

| CONTENT | ACCA (including FFA,FAB,FMA) | | FIA (excluding FFA,FAB,FMA) | |
|---|---|---|---|---|
| | Text | Kit | Text | Kit |
| Eletronic version of the book | ✓ | ✓ | ✓ | ✓ |
| Check Your Understanding Test with instant answers | ✓ | | | |
| Material updates | ✓ | ✓ | ✓ | ✓ |
| Latest official ACCA exam questions* | | ✓ | | |
| Extra question assistance using the signpost icon** | | ✓ | | |
| Timed questions with an online tutor debrief using clock icon*** | | ✓ | | |
| Interim assessment including questions and answers | ✓ | | ✓ | |
| Technical answers | ✓ | ✓ | ✓ | ✓ |

* Excludes F1, F2, F3, F4, FAB, FMA and FFA; for all other papers includes a selection of questions, as released by ACCA

** For ACCA P1-P7 only

*** Excludes F1, F2, F3, F4, FAB, FMA and FFA

### How to access your online resources

Kaplan Financial students will already have a MyKaplan account and these extra resources will be available to you online. You do not need to register again, as this process was completed when you enrolled. If you are having problems accessing online materials, please ask your course administrator.

If you are not studying with Kaplan and did not purchase your book via a Kaplan website, to unlock your extra online resources please go to www.mykaplan.co.uk/addabook (even if you have set up an account and registered books previously). You will then need to enter the ISBN number (on the title page and back cover) and the unique pass key number contained in the scratch panel below to gain access.

You will also be required to enter additional information during this process to set up or confirm your account details.

If you purchased through Kaplan Flexible Learning or via the Kaplan Publishing website you will automatically receive an e-mail invitation to MyKaplan. Please register your details using this email to gain access to your content. If you do not receive the e-mail or book content, please contact Kaplan Publishing.

### Your Code and Information

This code can only be used once for the registration of one book online. This registration and your online content will expire when the final sittings for the examinations covered by this book have taken place. Please allow one hour from the time you submit your book details for us to process your request.

Please scratch the film to access your MyKaplan code.

Please be aware that this code is case-sensitive and you will need to include the dashes within the passcode, but not when entering the ISBN. For further technical support, please visit www.MyKaplan.co.uk

KAPLAN PUBLISHING

# INTRODUCTORY LEVEL

## Paper MA1

---

# Management Information

---

## EXAM KIT

KAPLAN PUBLISHING

A catalogue record for this book is available from the British Library.

Published by Kaplan Publishing UK
Unit 2 The Business Centre
Molly Millars Lane
Wokingham
Berkshire
RG41 2QZ

ISBN 978-1-78740-055-9



Printed and bound in Great Britain

***Acknowledgements***

We are grateful to the Association of Chartered Certified Accountants, the Chartered Institute of Management Accountants and the Institute of Chartered Accountants in England and Wales for permission to reproduce past examination questions. The answers have been prepared by Kaplan Publishing.

# INTRODUCTION

Packed with exam-type questions, this book will help you to successfully prepare for your exam.

- In this exam kit you will find questions that are of exam standard and format – this will check and further develop your subject knowledge, as well as enable you to master the examination techniques.
- A mock exam is at the back of the book – try it under timed conditions and this will give you an idea of the way you will be tested in your actual exam.
- All questions are grouped by syllabus topics

Real exams for FIA MA1 are not published as questions are reused.

# CONTENTS



Quality and accuracy are of the utmost importance to us so if you spot an error in any of our products, please send an email to mykaplanreporting@kaplan.com with full details.

Our Quality Co-ordinator will work with our technical team to verify the error and take action to ensure it is corrected in future editions.

# INDEX TO QUESTIONS AND ANSWERS

## MULTIPLE-CHOICE QUESTIONS

# SYLLABUS AND REVISION GUIDANCE

## Syllabus content

No prior knowledge is required before commencing study for Paper MA1.

Candidates require a sound understanding of the methods and techniques covered in this paper to enable them to move on to the more complex systems and management control problems covered at subsequent levels.

Some of the methods introduced in this paper are revisited and extended in Paper MA2.

**DETAILED SYLLABUS**

A THE NATURE AND PURPOSE OF COST AND MANAGEMENT ACCOUNTING
Chapters 1 and 2

1 Nature of business organisation and accounting systems
2 Management information

B SOURCE DOCUMENTS AND CODING
Chapters 4-7

1 Sources of information
2 Coding system

C COST CLASSIFICATION AND MEASUREMENT
Chapter 3, 8 and 10

1 Cost classification
2 Cost units, cost centres, profit centres and investment centres

D RECORDING COSTS
Chapters 5,6,7 and 9

1 Accounting for materials
2 Accounting for labour
3 Accounting for other expenses
4 Accounting for product costs

E THE SPREADSHEET SYSTEM
Chapter 11

1 Spreadsheets overview
2 Creating and using spreadsheets
3 Presenting and printing spreadsheet data/information

**Key areas of the syllabus**

All areas of the syllabus are equally important.

## Planning your revision

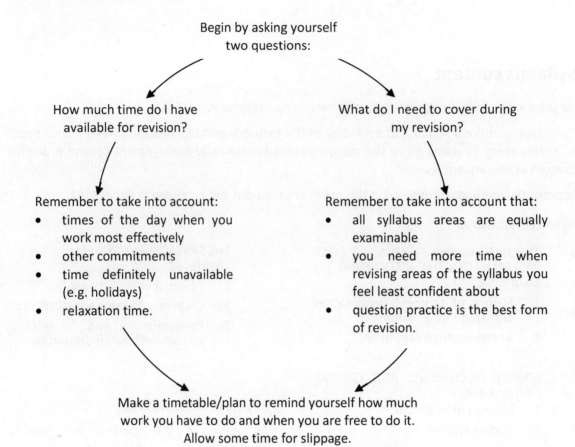

Begin by asking yourself two questions:

How much time do I have available for revision?

Remember to take into account:

- times of the day when you work most effectively
- other commitments
- time definitely unavailable (e.g. holidays)
- relaxation time.

What do I need to cover during my revision?

Remember to take into account that:

- all syllabus areas are equally examinable
- you need more time when revising areas of the syllabus you feel least confident about
- question practice is the best form of revision.

Make a timetable/plan to remind yourself how much work you have to do and when you are free to do it. Allow some time for slippage.

## Revision techniques

- Go through your notes and textbook **highlighting the important points.**
- You might want to produce your own set of **summarised notes.**
- **List key words** for each topic to remind you of the essential concepts.
- **Practise exam-standard questions**, under timed conditions.
- **Rework questions** that you got completely wrong the first time, but only when you think you know the subject better.
- If you get stuck on topics, **find someone to explain** them to you (your tutor or a colleague, for example).
- **Read recent articles** on the ACCA website or in the student magazine.
- **Read** good newspapers and professional journals.

# THE EXAMINATION

## Format of the exam

You can sit this exam as a paper-based or computer-based exam.

| | *Number of marks* |
|---|---|
| 50 multiple-choice questions (2 marks each) | 100 |
| Time allowed: 2 hours | |

## Answering the questions

- **Multiple choice questions** – read the questions carefully and work through any calculations required.
- **If you don't know the answer**, eliminate those options you know are incorrect and see if the answer becomes more obvious. Remember that only one answer to a multiple choice question can be right!
- **If you get stuck with a question** skip it and return to it later.
- **Answer every question** – if you do not know the answer, you do not lose anything by guessing. Towards the end of the examination spend the last five minutes reading through your answers and making any corrections.
- **Equally divide the time** you spend on questions. In a two-hour examination that has 50 questions you have about 2.4 minutes per a question.
- **Do not skip any part of the syllabus** and make sure that you have *learnt* definitions, *know* key words and their meanings and importance, and *understand* the names and meanings of rules, concepts and theories.
- Bear in mind that this paper is biased towards narrative rather than computational questions, essentially testing knowledge rather than application.

## Computer-based examinations

- Be sure you understand how to use the **software** before you start the exam. If in doubt, ask the assessment centre staff to explain it to you.
- Questions are **displayed on the screen** and answers are entered using keyboard and mouse. At the end of the exam, you are given a certificate showing the result you have achieved.
- **Don't panic** if you realise you've answered a question incorrectly – you can always go back and change your answer.

Section 1

# MULTIPLE CHOICE QUESTIONS

## THE NATURE AND PURPOSE OF COST AND MANAGEMENT ACCOUNTING

**1 Which of the following features are characteristic of an integrated accounting system?**

1 Management accounting and financial accounting ledger accounts are held in the same ledger.

2 There are no individual ledger accounts for receivables or payables.

3 Transactions are coded for both financial accounting purposes and management accounting purposes.

A 1 only

B 1 and 2 only

C 1 and 3 only

D 2 and 3 only

**2 Which of the following qualities is *not necessarily* a quality of good information?**

A It should be relevant

B It should be understandable

C It should be worth more than it costs to produce

D It should be available quickly

**3 Which of the following definitions best describes 'information'?**

A Data that consists of facts and statistics before they have been processed.

B Data that consists of numbers, letters, symbols, events and transactions which have been recorded but not yet processed into a form that is suitable for making decisions.

C Facts that have been summarised but not yet processed into a form that is suitable for making decisions.

D Data that has been processed in such a way that it has a meaning to the person who receives it, who may then use it to improve the quality of decision making.

4 **Which of the following is *not* a purpose of management information in a company?**

A To provide records of current and actual performance

B To compare actual performance with planned performance

C To help management with decision making

D To inform customers about the company's products

5 **Which of the following is *not* correct?**

A Cost accounting can be used for inventory valuation to meet the requirements of internal reporting only

B Management accounting provides appropriate information for decision making, planning, control and performance evaluation

C Routine information can be used for both short-term and long-run decisions

D Financial accounting information can be used for internal reporting purposes

6 **Which of the following are *all* qualities of good management information?**

A Digital, brief, relevant

B Reliable, consistent, timely

C Secure, accurate, printed

D Accessible, universal, complete

7 **Which of the following statements is *incorrect*?**

A Management accounting reports are more accurate than financial accounting statements.

B Management accounting reports are more detailed than financial accounting statements.

C Management accounting reports are more frequent than financial accounting statements.

D Management accounting reports are not disclosed to shareholders and investors.

8 **Which one of the following is always a quality of good information?**

A Immediate availability

B Availability to everyone

C Reliable

D Technically accurate

9 **Which one of the following statements is correct?**

A Data is held on computer in digital form whereas information is in a form that is readable to human beings.

B Information is obtained by processing data.

C Data and information mean the same thing.

D Data consists of numerical or statistical items of information.

**10 Which of the following items of information might be produced by a management accounting system?**

A Income tax deducted from employees' wages and salaries

B Amounts of money owed to suppliers

C Current bank balance

D Profitability of product items

**11 Which of the following is an example of external information that could be used in a management accounting system?**

A Consumer price index statistics

B Price list for the products sold by the business

C Production volume achieved by the production department

D Discounts given to customers

**12 Which of the following is *not* management accounting information?**

A Sales budget

B Variance report

C Payroll report

D Profitability report

**13 Which of the following items would be included in the financial accounting system but not in the management accounting system?**

A Sales commissions payable to sales representatives

B Costs of repairs to the office air conditioning system

C Profits paid out in dividends to the business owners

D Direct labour costs

**14 Why is management information valuable for decision making?**

A It enables management to make the correct decision

B It helps management to reach a more informed decision

C It can be used to allocate blame if a poor decision is made

D It enables managers to make decisions more quickly

**15 Which of the following statements about office manuals is *not* correct?**

A They are particularly useful for dealing with out-of-the-ordinary situations

B They can be used to check on the correct procedures in cases of doubt

C They can be used to help with the training of new staff

D They help to maintain standards of performance

**16 What is a prime entry record in an accounting system?**

A A record of an important transaction, usually a high-value transaction

B An entry in the ledger accounts

C The first record of a transaction entered into the accounting system

D A record of direct materials, direct labour and direct expenses costs

**17 Which of the following statements are correct?**

1 In a system of interlocking accounts, financial accounts and management accounts are recorded in the same ledger.

2 The number of errors in a computerised accounting system should be less than if a manual accounting system is used.

3 Transactions should be recorded more quickly in a computerised accounting system than in a manual accounting system.

A Statements 1 and 2 only are correct

B Statements 1 and 3 only are correct

C Statement 2 only is correct

D Statements 2 and 3 only are correct

**18 Which of the following best describes double entry bookkeeping?**

A A manual system of recording accounting transactions

B A system of recording business transactions in ledgers

C A system of recording an accounting transaction twice in the main ledger

D A system of management accounting

**19 Which of the following would be classified as data?**

A Number of purchase requisitions

B Analysis of wages into direct and indirect costs

C Table showing variances from budget

D Graph showing the number of labour hours worked

**20 Which of the following are primary data?**

(i) Information on timesheets used for making up wages.

(ii) Information from a government publication concerning forecast inflation rates used for budgeting.

(iii) Information from a trade publication used to choose a supplier of raw materials.

A (i) and (ii)

B (i) and (iii)

C (i) only

D (i), (ii) and (iii)

**21 Which of the following is a feature of financial accounting information?**

A It is used to calculate the cost of a product or service

B Limited companies are required by law to prepare this information

C It is concerned with future results as well as historical information

D The benefit must exceed the cost and it must be relevant for purpose

**22 What is the scientific term for facts, figures and information?**

A Consultancy

B Data

C Referencing

D Statistics

**23 Which one of the following is true with regard to management information?**

A It is the same as operating information

B It must be produced by a computer

C It should be completely accurate, regardless of cost

D It should be produced if its cost is less than the increased revenue to which it leads

**24 Which one of the following is an example of internal information for the wages department of a large company?**

A A Code of Practice issued by the Institute of Directors

B A new national minimum wage

C Changes to tax coding arrangements issued by the tax authorities

D The company's employees' schedule of hours worked

**25 Which one of the following would be included in the financial accounts, but may be excluded from the cost accounts?**

A Bank interest and charges

B Depreciation of storeroom handling equipment

C Direct material costs

D Factory manager's salary

**26 What is the most appropriate definition of an office?**

A A centre for exchanging information between businesses

B A centre for information and administration

C A place where information is stored

D A room where many people using IT work

**27 Which one of the following is a disadvantage of office manuals?**

A Strict interpretation of instructions creates inflexibility

B The quality of service received from suppliers is reduced

C They create bureaucracy and demotivate staff

D They do not facilitate the induction and training of new staff

**28 Which one of the following is least likely to be carried out by an Accounts Department?**

A Arrangement of payment of payables

B Calculation of wages and salaries to be paid

C Despatch of customer orders

D Preparation of company financial records

**29 What is the main purpose of prime entry records?**

A to calculate the cash received and spent by a business

B to prevent a large volume of unnecessary detail in the ledgers

C to provide a monthly check on the double entry bookkeeping

D to separate the transactions subject to sales tax from those that are exempt

# SOURCE DOCUMENTS AND CODING

**30 Which of the following is usually responsible for preparing a delivery note?**

A Buyer

B Supplier

C Stores manager

D Accountant

**31 Which of the following is in the correct chronological sequence for sales documents?**

A Enquiry – Order – Invoice – Payment

B Order – Enquiry – Invoice – Payment

C Enquiry – Order – Payment – Invoice

D Enquiry – Invoice – Order – Payment

**32 Which of the following is in the correct chronological sequence for purchase documents?**

A Purchase order – Invoice – Goods received note – Delivery note

B Delivery note – Goods received note – Purchase order – Invoice

C Purchase order – Delivery note – Goods received note – Invoice

D Goods received note – Delivery note – Purchase order – Invoice

**33 Which of the following documents should be checked before a purchase invoice is paid, to confirm that the price and quantities are correct?**

| | *Price check* | *Quantity check* |
|---|---|---|
| A | Purchase order | Purchase order |
| B | Goods received note | Delivery note |
| C | Purchase invoice | Goods received note |
| D | Purchase order | Goods received note |

**34** You are the accountant responsible for the input into the computer accounting system of data about goods received from suppliers. For each transaction, you require a copy of the purchase order, delivery note, goods received note and invoice.

**Where are you most likely to find the code number for an item of inventory for entering in the system?**

A Purchase order

B Delivery note

C Goods received note

D Invoice

**35 Which one of the following is *least* likely to be carried out by the accounts department?**

A Collecting money receivable from credit customers

B Receiving goods from suppliers into store

C Processing expenses claims

D Arranging payments of tax to the tax authorities

**36** Hockey Skill operates from three main sites. In analysing its costs (overheads) it uses a nine digit coding system. A sample from the coding manual shows:

| *Site* | | *Expenditure type* | | *Function* | |
|---|---|---|---|---|---|
| Whitby | 100 | Rent | 410 | Purchasing | 600 |
| Scarborough | 200 | Power | 420 | Finance | 610 |
| York | 300 | Heat and light | 430 | Production | 620 |
| | | Travel costs | 500 | Sales | 630 |
| | | Telephone and postage | 520 | | |

The order of coding is: site/expense/function

**How would an invoice for the Whitby site for power be coded?**

A 100/420/600

B 100/420/620

C 100/420/610

D 100/430/610

**37** In accounting systems, data is usually organised using codes.

**Which one of the following statements about codes is *incorrect*?**

A Using codes helps to improve the speed and accuracy of data processing.

B Using codes allows more data validation checks to be carried out.

C A hierarchical code structure makes it easier to find items on a code list, since similar items are grouped.

D Codes in accounting reduce the need for accountants to understand the principles of accounting.

**38** A firm uses a unique code to identify each customer and customer account. The code consists of the first three letters of the customer's name, followed by four digits.

**Which one of the following will appear first when the customers are sorted into descending order?**

A TRO1100

B TRO1214

C TOP1213

D TOR1102

**39** Inventory codes used by an organisation are eight-digit numerical codes. Inventory records are held on computer in a real-time inventory control system.

**Which of the following measures is most likely to prevent errors with the input of the inventory code number for each inventory transaction?**

A Existence check

B Dual input of the inventory code

C Verification check

D Check digit check

**40** A firm uses a unique code to identify each customer – the first four letters of each name are followed by four digits.

**Which one of the following will appear first when customers are sorted into descending order?**

A ADAM0001

B ADAA0099

C ADDA0100

D ABAB0999

**41 Which one of the following is the correct sequential flow of documents to complete the purchase of goods on credit?**

A Goods received note, purchase order, cheque requisition, invoice, delivery note

B Purchase order, delivery note, goods received note, invoice, cheque requisition

C Purchase order, goods received note, delivery note, cheque requisition, invoice

D Purchase order, invoice, goods received note, cheque requisition, delivery note

**42 Which member of staff is most likely to raise a goods received note?**

A Delivery driver

B Finance director

C Sales ledger clerk

D Store clerk

**43 Who is most likely to record deliveries into stores?**

A Stores clerk

B Sales clerk

C Accounts clerk

D Personnel assistant

**44 Which of the following describes a purchase order?**

A Issued by the purchasing department, sent to the supplier requesting materials.

B Issued by the stores department, sent to the purchasing department requesting materials.

C Received together with the materials and compared to the materials received.

D Issued by the production department, sent to the stores department requesting materials.

## COST CLASSIFICATION AND MEASUREMENT

**45 Which costs are included within a prime cost?**

A All variable costs

B Direct labour and material only

C Direct labour, direct material and direct expense

D Direct labour, direct material and production overhead

**46 Which of the following statements best describes a semi-variable cost?**

A A cost that increases in direct proportion to output

B A cost that remains constant irrespective of the level of output

C A cost that contains an element of both fixed and variable cost

D A cost that increases throughout the year

**47 Which of the costs listed below is *not* a fixed cost?**

A Insurance

B Business rates

C Depreciation – based on straight-line method

D Materials used in production

**48 Which costs are included within production overheads?**

A Variable overheads only

B Indirect labour, indirect material and indirect expenses related to production activity

C Indirect expenses only

D Indirect labour and material related to the production activity

**49 Which of the following statements best describes a direct cost?**

A A cost which cannot be influenced by its budget holder

B Expenditure which can be economically identified with a specific cost unit

C A cost which needs to be apportioned to a cost centre

D The highest proportion of the total cost of a product

**50 What would be the most appropriate cost unit for a cake manufacturer?**

A Cake

B Batch

C Kilogram

D Production run

**51 A factory makes wooden chairs.**

**Which of the following items would be most likely to behave as stepped costs?**

A Wood used to make chairs

B Factory supervisors' salaries

C Heating and light costs

D Staples to fix the fabric to the seat of the chair

**52 The following graph represents which type of cost?**

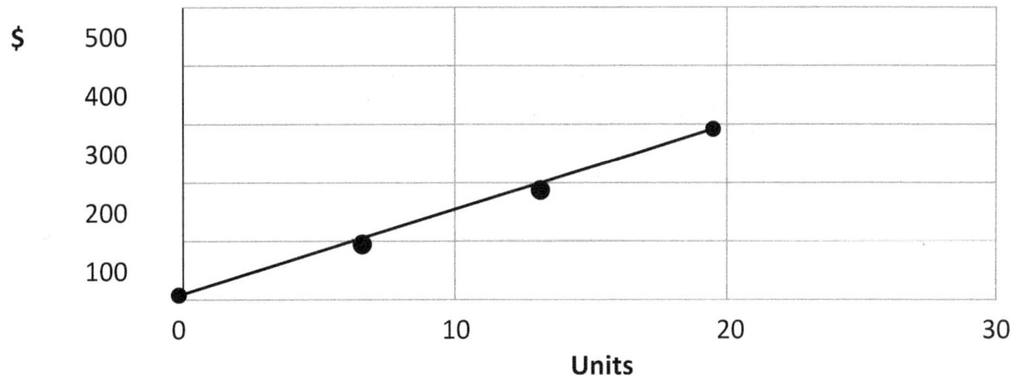


A Fixed cost

B Variable cost

C Semi-variable cost

D Stepped cost

**53 For operational purposes, for a company operating a fleet of delivery vehicles, which of the following methods of calculating cost would be most useful?**

A Cost per mile run

B Cost per driver hour

C Cost per tonne mile

D Cost per kilogram carried

**54** The following data relate to the overhead expenditure of contract cleaners at two activity levels:

| | | |
|---|---|---|
| Square metres cleaned | 12,750 | 15,100 |
| Overheads | \$73,950 | \$83,585 |

**If fixed overheads are estimated to cost \$21,675, what is the estimated overhead cost if 16,200 square metres are to be cleaned?**

A \$66,420

B \$88,095

C \$89,674

D \$93,960

**55** The following data relate to two output levels of a department:

| | | |
|---|---|---|
| Machine hours | 17,000 | 18,500 |
| Overheads | $246,500 | $251,750 |

**What is the amount of fixed overheads?**

A $5,250

B $59,500

C $187,000

D $246,500

**56** **Which of the following is a direct expense?**

A Materials used on production

B Special tools for job 721

C Power

D Depreciation

**57** Hockey Skill manufactures hockey sticks. A summary of some cost headings include:

(a) wood used as raw material

(b) rubber covers for handles

(c) depreciation

(d) power

(e) sales manager's salary

(f) labour in assembly department

(g) oils and greases

(h) telephone and postage

(i) insurance of plant

(j) supervisory labour.

**Which of the above items would be classified as production overheads?**

A (a), (f), (d) and (e)

B (c), (d), (g), (i) and (j)

C (e), (h), (i) and (j)

D (a), (b), (c), (d) and (f)

**58** A small engineering company that makes generators specifically to customers' own designs has had to purchase some special tools for a particular job. The tools will have no further use after the work has been completed and will be scrapped.

**How should the cost of these tools be treated?**

A Variable production overheads

B Fixed production overheads

C Indirect expenses

D Direct expenses

**59 Which of the following statements best describes a cost centre?**

A A unit of product or service for which costs are calculated

B An amount of profit attributable to an activity

C A function or location within an organisation for which costs are accumulated

D A section of the organisation for which budgets are prepared and control is exercised

**60 For which of the following types of business unit would residual income be a suitable measure of performance?**

A Cost centre

B Revenue centre

C Profit centre

D Investment centre

**61 Which of the following is a service cost centre in a manufacturing company?**

A Finishing

B Machining

C Despatch

D Assembly

**62** A transport company has a cost accounting system for measuring the costs of the services it provides. The company provides train services throughout the southern region of the country.

**Which of the following would be the most appropriate cost unit for measuring operating costs, in a way that costs of its various services can be usefully compared?**

A Cost per train

B Cost per journey

C Cost per passenger

D Cost per passenger/kilometre

**63** A training company runs courses for students that vary in length between one day and four weeks. The size of classes varies between 5 students and 40 students. The company wants to set a price for its courses based on a mark-up on cost.

**What would be the most appropriate basis for measuring costs?**

A Cost per student per day

B Cost per course

C Cost per student

D Cost per day

**64** A law firm provides a range of services to clients, who are a mixture of business, government and private clients. It has offices in three cities in different parts of the country. The firm's senior partners are reviewing the range of services the firm provides, with a view to specialising more in the future.

**How might the firm best analyse its profitability for this purpose?**

A Profitability of each office

B Profitability of each type of service provided

C Profitability of each type of client

D Profitability of each employee

**65 Which of the following statements is correct about costs in a manufacturing business?**

A The fixed cost per unit is the same at all levels of output

B The fixed cost per unit falls as output increases, at a constant rate

C The fixed cost per unit falls as output increases, at a declining rate

D The fixed cost per unit falls as output increases, at an increasing rate

**66 Which of the following is most likely to be treated as an indirect cost by a house builder?**

A Nails and screws

B Windows

C Bricks

D Electricity cables

**67** A travel company offers holidays to a range of destinations, which it advertises in a single brochure. Customers are transported to their destination in flights booked by the company for its exclusive use. Within each holiday destination, the company offers accommodation at different hotels, ranging from two-star to five-star hotels. The company measures the profitability of holidays to each hotel at each destination.

**Which of the following would be the direct costs of a holiday at the Hotel Splendide in Trinidad?**

(i) Brochure production and printing costs

(ii) Air charter flight costs

(iii) Hotel accommodation costs

A (i) and (iii) only

B (i) and (ii) only

C (ii) and (iii) only

D (iii) only

**68** **What is the full production cost per unit of a manufactured product?**

A Direct material cost plus direct labour cost per unit

B Prime cost plus production overhead cost per unit

C Prime cost plus variable production overhead per unit

D Production overhead cost per unit

**69** **Which one of the following statements is true?**

A Heating costs are a variable cost because they differ according to the season of the year.

B A semi-variable cost is fixed for a certain level of activity and then changes to a new fixed level.

C The fixed cost per unit of output decreases as output increases.

D Total variable costs are constant at all levels of output.

**70** The following costs are recorded for different levels of production:

| | *Period 1* | *Period 2* | *Period 3* |
|---|---|---|---|
| Costs | $1,400 | $1,600 | $1,600 |
| Units of production | 200 | 300 | 400 |

**This cost could be classified as:**

A fixed

B variable

C semi-variable

D stepped

**71 Which of the following costs would be classified as an indirect cost?**

A Flour for baking bread

B Invoice for icing a wedding cake

C Wages cost of baker

D Depreciation of ovens

**72** The following charts demonstrate various costs in relation to activity:

Chart 1

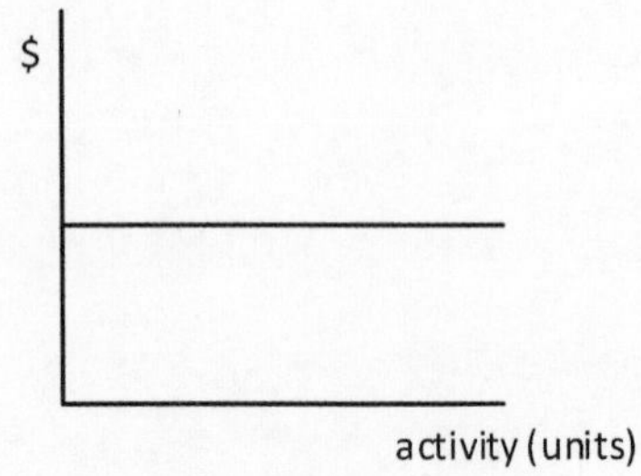


Chart 2

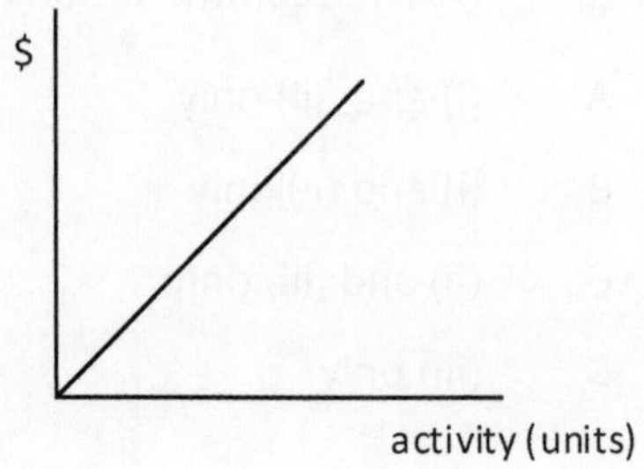


Chart 3

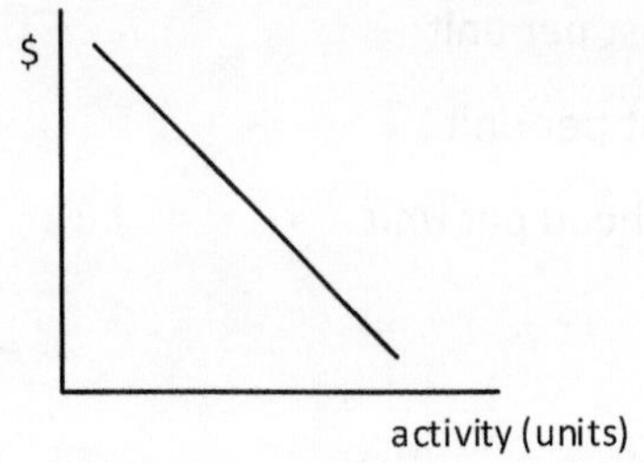


Chart 4

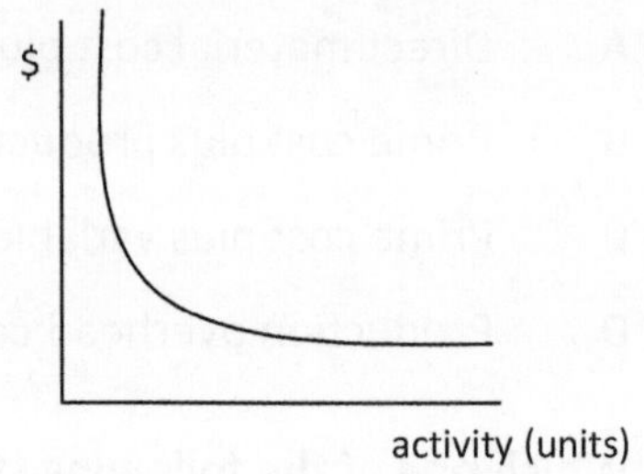


**Which of the above charts represents variable cost per unit?**

A Chart 1

B Chart 2

C Chart 3

D Chart 4

**73 Which one of the following departments is *not* a service cost centre in a manufacturing company?**

A Accounting

B Assembly

C Maintenance

D Personnel

**74** A company operates a retail supermarket chain selling a range of grocery and household products. It has branches throughout the country and is reviewing the range of goods to be stocked in each of these branches.

**How might the company best analyse its profitability for this purpose?**

A By area of the country

B By contract with each supplier

C By customer payment method

D By product line stocked

**75** A company produces electronic circuit boards. Each circuit board has a raw material input of $60 and labour input that costs $20. The company intends to produce 1,000 circuit boards per week. The company must also pay the rent of the factory totalling $20,000 per annum, business rates of $4,000 per annum and the production director's salary of $24,000 per annum.

**What is the fixed cost of the business?**

A $20,000

B $24,000

C $48,000

D $80,000

**76** A large hotel has coffee shops, restaurants and banqueting. They are used by hotel residents and outside users. The manager of the hotel is responsible for encouraging residents to use the hotel's catering facilities.

**Which report will show how effective the manager has been in achieving this objective?**

A A report analysing the utilisation of hotel catering services per room occupied

B A report showing the amount of money spent in the hotel's catering facilities

C A report showing the number of residents in the hotel at any given time

D A report showing the occupancy of the various catering facilities

**77** **Which description best fits the cost curve below?**

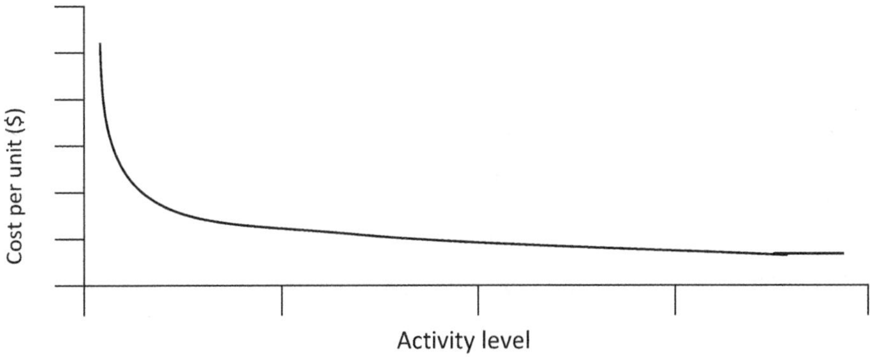


A Direct labour cost per unit

B Direct material cost per unit

C Fixed production cost per unit

D Variable production cost per unit

**78 Which one of the following items is most likely to be treated as an indirect cost by a furniture manufacturer?**

A Fabric to cover the seat of a chair

B Metal used for the legs of a chair

C Staples to fit the fabric to the seat of a chair

D Wood used to make the frame of a chair

**79** The Rendez-Vous is a hotel, the following are either cost centres or cost units for a hotel:

(a) Bar

(b) Restaurant

(c) Room/night

(d) Meal served

(e) Conference delegate

(f) Fitness suite

(g) Conference room

**Which of the above items would be classified as cost units?**

A (a), (c), (d) and (f)

B (b), (d) and (g)

C (e), (f) and (g)

D (c), (d) and (e)

**80 Please identify the following as either cost centres or cost units for a house building company:**

(i) Quantity surveying

(ii) Planning

(iii) Bungalow

(iv) Town House

(v) Design

(vi) Sales

(vii) Detached House

| | *Cost centre* | *cost unit* |
|---|---|---|
| A | (ii), (iii) and (iv) | (i), (v), (vi) and (vii) |
| B | (i), (ii), (v) and (vi) | (iii), (iv) and (vii) |
| C | (i), (iii) and (vii) | (ii), (iv), (v) and (vi) |
| D | (v), (vi) and (vii) | (i), (ii), (iii) and (iv) |

**81 When preparing an operating statement based on marginal costing principles, inventory valuation comprises which of the following costs?**

A Direct labour and material only

B Prime cost plus production overhead

C Prime cost plus variable production overhead

D Total cost of sales

# COST ACCOUNTING

**82** RCW operates a bonus scheme based on time saved against a predetermined time allowance for actual output. Employees are typically expected to produce 700 units a week. The standard allowance is 20 units of 'R' per hour. In Week 6, an operative produced 750 units of 'R' in 32 hours.

**What is the time saved by this employee in Week 6 on 'R' production?**

A 2.50

B 3.00

C 5.50

D 5.90

**83 Gross wages incurred in a cost centre for the month of January totalled $45,250, as follows:**

| | | $ |
|---|---|---|
| Ordinary time | direct employees | 27,500 |
| | indirect employees | 6,500 |
| Overtime | direct employees | |
| | basic | 4,500 |
| | premium | 2,250 |
| Special conditions allowance | direct employees | 1,300 |
| | indirect employees | 450 |
| Shift allowance | direct employees | 2,000 |
| Sick pay | direct employees | 750 |

The overtime is a regular feature.

**What is the correct figure for direct wages for January?**

A $31,550

B $32,800

C $35,300

D $32,000

**84** HH operates an incentive scheme based on differential piecework. Employees are paid on the following basis:

| | | | |
|---|---|---|---|
| Weekly output up to: | 600 units | – | $0.40 per unit |
| | 601–650 units | – | $0.50 per unit |
| | 650 units + | – | $0.75 per unit |

This is paid only upon production meeting quality standards with only the additional units qualifying for the higher rates. In Week 17, an employee produced 670 units, of which 10 were rejected.

**What would the gross pay for the week be?**

A $272.50

B $280.00

C $330.00

D $495.00

**85** **Which of the following methods of remuneration is NOT an incentive-based scheme?**

A Straight piecework

B High day rate

C Group bonus

D Differential piecework

**86** **Which of the following relates to the cost of replacing (rather than retaining) labour due to high employee turnover?**

A Improving working conditions

B Suffering the learning curve effect

C Provision of a pension

D Provision of welfare services

**87** A job requires 2,400 actual labour hours for completion and it is anticipated that there will be 20% idle time.

**If the wage rate is $10 per hour, what is the budgeted labour cost for the job?**

A $19,200

B $24,000

C $28,800

D $30,000

**88** A job is budgeted to require 3,300 productive hours after incurring 25% idle time.

**If the total labour cost budgeted for the job is $36,300, what is the labour cost per hour?**

A $8.25

B $8.80

C $11.00

D $13.75

**89** **Which *one* of the following would be classified as direct labour?**

A Personnel manager in a company servicing cars

B Bricklayer in a construction company

C General manager in a DIY shop

D Maintenance manager in a company producing cameras

**90** Employee A is a carpenter and normally works 36 hours per week. The standard rate of pay is $3.60 per hour. A premium of 50% of the basic hourly rate is paid for all overtime hours worked. During the last week of October 2001, Employee A worked for 42 hours. The overtime hours worked were for the following reasons:

| | |
|---|---|
| Machine breakdown: | 4 hours |
| To complete a special job at the request of the customer: | 2 hours |

**How much of Employee A's earnings for the last week of October would have been treated as direct wages?**

A $162.00

B $129.60

C $140.40

D $151.20

**91** An employee is paid on a piecework basis. The basis of the piecework scheme is as follows:

1 to 100 units – $0.40 per unit

101 to 200 units – $0.50 per unit

201 to 299 units – $0.60 per unit

with only the additional units qualifying for the higher rates. Rejected units do not qualify for payment.

During a particular day the employee produced 240 units of which 8 were rejected as faulty.

**What did the employee earn for the day's work?**

A $109.20

B $114.00

C $139.20

D $144.00

**92 Which of the following is usually classed as a step cost?**

A Supervisor's wages

B Raw materials

C Rates

D Telephone

**93 Which of the following would be most likely to provide Information on contracted rates of pay?**

A a trade union

B a production manager

C a personnel manager

D a work study manager

**94 Which of the following statements is correct?**

A Idle time cannot be controlled because it is always due to external factors

B Idle time is always controllable because it is due to internal factors

C Idle time is always due to inefficient production staff

D Idle time is not always the fault of production staff

**95** A company operates a piecework scheme to pay its staff. The staff receive $0.20 for each unit produced. However the company guarantees that every member of staff receive at least $15 per day.

Shown below is the number of units produced by Operator A during a recent week:

| *Day* | *Monday* | *Tuesday* | *Wednesday* | *Thursday* | *Friday* |
|---|---|---|---|---|---|
| Units produced | 90 | 70 | 75 | 60 | 90 |

**What are Operator A's earnings for the week?**

A $75.00

B $77.00

C $81.00

D $152.00

**96 Which of the following statements best describes overhead allocation?**

A The charging of overhead to cost units

B The allotment of proportions of items of cost to cost centres or cost units

C The charging of direct material to jobs

D The allotment of whole items of indirect cost to cost centres

**97** A method of dealing with overheads involves spreading common costs over cost centres on the basis of benefit received.

**What is this method known as?**

A Overhead absorption

B Overhead apportionment

C Overhead allocation

D Overhead analysis

**98** Production supervisory salaries are classed as production overhead.

**Which is the most appropriate basis of apportioning this cost to cost centres?**

A Number of units produced

B Machine hours

C Direct labour hours

D Number of machines

**99 Which of the following would be the most appropriate basis for apportioning machinery insurance costs to cost centres within a factory?**

A The number of machines in each cost centre

B The floor area occupied by the machinery in each cost centre

C The value of the machinery in each cost centre

D The operating hours of the machinery in each cost centre

**100 Factory overheads can be absorbed by which of the following methods?**

1 Direct labour hours

2 Machine hours

3 Indirect labour hours

4 $x per unit

A 1, 2, 3 or 4

B 1 and 2 only

C 1, 2 or 4 only

D 2, 3 or 4 only

**101** A business employs two grades of labour in its production department. Grade A workers are considered direct labour employees, and are paid $10 per hour. Grade B workers are considered indirect labour employees, and are paid $6 per hour.

In the week just ended, Grade A labour worked 30 hours of overtime, 10 hours on a specific customer order at the customer's request, and the other 20 hours as general overtime. Grade B labour worked 45 hours of overtime, as general overtime. Overtime is paid at time-and-one-half.

**What would be the total amount of pay for overtime worked in the week that is considered to be a direct labour cost?**

A $50

B $150

C $285

D $350

**102** A manufacturing business is currently extremely busy and overtime is being worked.

**How would the cost of the overtime premium payable to direct labour employees normally be treated?**

A a direct cost

B a production overhead cost

C an administration overhead cost

D a prime cost

**103** **Which one of the following would be classed as indirect labour?**

A Assembly workers in a firm that manufactures digital video recorders

B A stores assistant in a factory stores

C A plasterer in a building construction firm

D An audit clerk in a firm of auditors

**104** **What is cost apportionment?**

A Charging discrete, identifiable items of cost to cost centres or cost units.

B The collection of costs attributable to cost centres and cost units using the costing methods applied by the business.

C The process of establishing the costs of cost centres or cost units.

D The division of a cost between two or more cost centres in proportion to the estimated benefit received by each centre.

**105** A manufacturer employs two grades of labour in its machining department, grade A and grade B. Grade A employees are treated as direct labour employees and grade B employees are treated as indirect labour employees. Grade A employees are paid $8 per hour and grade B workers receive $6 per hour. The basic working week is 40 hours. Overtime is paid at time + 50%, to all employees in the department. There are 10 grade A employees and 6 grade B employees.

During a particular week, each grade A employee worked for 45 hours and each grade B employee worked for 43 hours. The overtime was necessary due to staff sickness.

**What will be the charge to production overhead for the week?**

A $54

B $254

C $1,602

D $1,802

**106** The payroll department has produced the following information for the month about the pay for employees in department X.

| Department X | $ |
|---|---|
| Payments to employees | 7,500 |
| Income tax | 2,500 |
| Employees' state benefit contributions (NI in the UK) | 1,200 |
| Employer's state benefit contributions (NI in the UK) | 2,000 |

**What are the gross wages for the department for the month?**

A $7,500

B $10,000

C $11,200

D $13,200

**107** The payroll department has produced the following information for the month about the pay for employees in department Z. Department Z is a part of the accounts division.

| Department Z | $ |
|---|---|
| Salaries (gross wages) | 23,000 |
| Income tax | 4,500 |
| Employees' state benefit contributions (NI in the UK) | 2,400 |
| Employer's state benefit contributions (NI in the UK) | 3,500 |

**What is the labour cost in Department Z that would be treated as administration overhead cost for the month?**

A $23,000

B $26,500

C $29,900

D $33,400

**108** An employee is paid on a stepped piecework basis, as follows:

| Units produced each week | $ |
|---|---|
| 1 – 200 | 0.60 per unit |
| 201 – 300 | 0.80 per unit |
| Over 301 | 1.00 per unit |

Only the additional units qualify for the higher rates. Rejected units do not qualify for any payment

During a particular week, the employee makes 380 units, of which 35 were rejected as faulty.

**What were his gross earnings for the week?**

A $245

B $280

C $345

D $380

**109 What would be the appropriate basis for apportioning the costs of heating and lighting between cost centres in a factory building?**

A Number of employees

B Number of machines

C Value of machinery

D Floor area occupied by each department

**110 What would be the appropriate basis for apportioning the factory manager's salary between cost centres in a factory building?**

A Number of employees

B Number of machines

C Value of machinery

D Floor area occupied by each department

**111** A business maintains an inventory control database. For each item of inventory, the file contains the quantity of free inventory for the item. For inventory item 245711, the current quantity held by the business is 400 units. The stores department has received requisitions from user departments for 320 units, which have yet to be processed and dealt with. An order for a new supply of 350 units has been placed with the supplier, and delivery is expected in one or two days.

**What is the quantity of free inventory for this item?**

A 30

B 370

C 400

D 430

**112** A company employs 20 direct production operatives and 10 indirect staff in its manufacturing department. The normal operating hours for all employees is 38 hours per week and all staff are paid a basic rate of $5 per hour. Overtime hours are paid at the basic rate + 50%. During a particular week all employees worked for 44 hours to meet the company's general production requirements.

**What amount would be charged to production overhead?**

A $300

B $450

C $2,350

D $2,650

**113 With which costs is absorption costing concerned?**

A Direct labour costs only

B Direct material costs only

C Fixed costs only

D Variable and fixed costs

**114** Aspects of payroll include:

1 Employer's state benefit contribution (National Insurance in the UK)

2 Employee's state benefit contribution (National Insurance in the UK)

3 Income tax (PAYE in the UK)

4 Salaries

**Which of the above are costs to an employer?**

A 1 and 4 only

B 2 and 4 only

C 2, 3 and 4 only

D 1, 2, 3 and 4

**115** An employee is paid on a piecework basis. The scheme is as follows:

| | |
|---|---|
| 1 – 100 units per day | $0.20 per unit |
| 101 – 200 units per day | $0.30 per unit |
| > 200 units per day | $0.40 per unit |

Only the additional units qualify for the higher rates. Rejected units do not qualify for payment. An employee produced 210 units in a day of which 17 were rejected as faulty.

**How much did the employee earn for the day?**

A $47.90

B $54.00

C $57.90

D $84.00

**116** **It is possible for an item of overhead expenditure to be shared amongst several cost centres. It is also possible that an item of overhead expenditure may relate to just one specific cost centre.**

**What term is used to describe charging an item of overhead to just one specific cost centre?**

A Absorption

B Allocation

C Apportionment

D Re-apportionment

**117** **What would be the most appropriate basis for apportioning machinery insurance costs to cost centres within a factory?**

A Floor area occupied by the machinery

B Number of machines

C Operating hours of machinery

D Value of machinery

**118** There are 275 units of material BX in stock. An order for 650 units is expected and a material requisition for 300 units has not yet been issued to the production cost centre.

**What is the free inventory?**

A 275 units

B 625 units

C 650 units

D 675 units

**119** A company employs 30 direct production staff and 15 indirect staff in its manufacturing department. The normal operating hours for all employees is 37 hours per week and all staff are paid a basic rate of $8 per hour. Overtime hours are paid at the basic rate + 50%. During a particular week all employees worked for 42 hours to meet the company's general production requirements.

**What is the total direct labour cost?**

A $8,880

B $10,080

C $10,680

D $10,980

**120** An employee is paid on a piecework basis. The scheme is as follows:

| | |
|---|---|
| 1 – 200 units per day | $0.15 per unit |
| 201 – 500 units per day | $0.20 per unit |
| > 500 units per day | $0.25 per unit |

Only the additional units qualify for the higher rates. Rejected units do not qualify for payment. An employee produced 512 units in a day of which 17 were rejected as faulty.

**What wage is paid to the employee?**

A $128

B $103

C $99

D $89

**121** It is expected that a product will take 36 minutes to produce. In a period 180 hours are worked and 325 units of product are made. A bonus of half of the time saved is paid to the employees. The wage rate is $8.00 per hour.

**What is the total amount of bonus paid to the employees?**

A $252

B $120

C $60

D None

**122** In a payments by results scheme employees are paid a bonus based on hours saved at the basic wage rate. The bonus payable to the employee is calculated as the hours saved multiplied by the ratio of time saved to time allowed.

An employee produces 480 units in 72 hours. The time allowed for this number of units is 108 hours. The employee's basic rate of pay is $10 per hour.

**What is the total amount payable to the employee for this job?**

A $120

B $720

C $733

D $840

**123** A company operates a job costing system. Job 812 requires $60 of direct materials, $40 of direct labour and $20 of direct expenses. Direct labour is paid $8 per hour. Production overheads are absorbed at a rate of $16 per direct labour hour and non-production overheads are absorbed at a rate of 60% of prime cost.

**What is the total cost of Job 812?**

A $240

B $260

C $272

D $320

**124 Which one of the following statements is incorrect?**

A Job costs are collected separately, whereas process costs are averages

B In job costing the progress of a job can be ascertained from the materials requisition notes and job tickets or time sheet

C In process costing information is needed about work passing through a process and work remaining in each process

D In process costing, but not job costing, the cost of normal loss will be incorporated into normal product costs

**125** A firm uses job costing and recovers overheads on a direct labour cost basis.

Two jobs were worked on during a period, the details of which were:

| | *Job 1* | *Job 2* | *Job 3* |
|---|---|---|---|
| | $ | $ | $ |
| Opening work-in-progress | 8,500 | 0 | 32,000 |
| Material in period | 17,150 | 29,025 | 5,675 |
| Labour for period | 12,500 | 23,000 | 4,500 |

The overheads for the period were exactly as budgeted, $140,000. Actual labour costs were also the same as budgeted.

Jobs 1 and 2 were the only incomplete jobs at the end of the period.

**What was the value of closing work-in-progress?**

A $81,900

B $90,175

C $140,675

D $214,425

**126** A firm uses job costing and recovers overheads at a rate of 350% of the direct labour cost.

Job 352 was completed during the period and consisted of 2,400 identical circuit boards. The firm adds 50% to total production costs to arrive at a selling price.

| The details of job 352 were: | $ |
|---|---|
| Opening work-in-progress | 46,000 |
| Material in period | 0 |
| Labour for period | 4,500 |

**What is the selling price of a circuit board?**

A It cannot be calculated without more information

B $31.56

C $41.41

D $58.33

570 228 ~~380 : 6 = 63,3~~

646 228

7,6

45 × 2 = 90

80 × 2,40 = 192

75 × 2,20 = 165 + 5 × 2,40 = 177

50 × 2 + 25 × 2,20 + 5 × 2,40 = 100 + 55 + 12 = 167

80 = 2

p.u. = 2,08

3 × 12 = 36

320 + 12 = 332

296 + 36 = 332

~~37 x 8 + 3 x 12 = 296 + 36 = 336~~

37 x 60 = 2220 min.

~~2220 : 54~~ =

2220 : 48 = 46,25.

2220 - 54 =

7,75 x 48 = 372/60

4,25

6,2 x 6,80 = 42,16.

~~52 700~~

~~12400~~

21,08.

~~56,389~~

52 700. 56 389

~~12 15~~

12400. 12648

~~4,4,4~~

~~10 x 11,1 = 111~~

~~3 x 14,80 = 44,4~~

Jack 35 x 7,40 = 259

66,6

331,7. 103,6

5 x 9,3 = 46,5

3 x 12,40 = 37,2

jeans 40 x 6,20 = 248

**127** A company uses process costing to value its output. The following was recorded for the period:

| | |
|---|---|
| Input materials | 2,000 units at $4.50 per unit |
| Conversion costs | $13,040 |
| Loss | 5% of input |

There were no opening or closing inventories.

**What was the valuation of one unit of output?**

A $11.80

B $11.60

C $11.20

D $11.00

**128** In a production process the percentage completion of the work-in-progress (WIP) at the end of a period is found to have been understated.

**When this is corrected what will be the effect on the cost per unit and the total value of the WIP?**

| | *Cost per unit* | *Total value of WIP* |
|---|---|---|
| A | Decrease | Decrease |
| B | Decrease | Increase |
| C | Increase | Decrease |
| D | Increase | Increase |

**129** The direct costs for batch number 35401, comprising 200 men's shirts, were as follows:

| | |
|---|---|
| Materials | $3,000 |
| Labour | 120 hours @$5 per hour |

Production overheads are absorbed at a company-wide rate of $12 per direct labour hour.

Non-production overheads are absorbed at the rate of $1,000 per batch.

**What is the total production cost per unit of each shirt in the batch?**

A $18.00

B $22.20

C $25.20

D $30.20

**130** ABG plc makes batches of 'own brand' ready meals for supermarkets, using a semi-automated production process. The costs for batch number 87102, comprising 10,000 Thai fish curry meals, were as follows:

| | |
|---|---|
| Ingredients | $7,000 |
| Packaging | $3,600 |
| Labour | 80 hours @$10 per hour |

The batch took 40 machine hours to produce.

Production overheads are absorbed at a factory-wide rate of $5 per machine hour.

Non-production overheads are absorbed at the rate of $15 per labour hour.

**What is the total cost per meal in the batch?**

A $1.16

B $1.22

C $1.28

D $1.30

**131** A company uses process costing to value its output. The following was recorded for the period:

| | |
|---|---|
| Input materials | 1,000 litres at $5 per litre |
| Conversion costs | $11,000 |
| Output | 800 litres, as expected. |

There were no opening or closing inventories.

**What was the valuation of one litre of output?**

A $5.00

B $16.00

C $18.75

D $20.00

**132** Procal Ltd is a manufacturer. In Period 1 the following production occurred

| | | |
|---|---|---|
| Units started (there was no opening WIP) | = | 1,300 units |
| Closing WIP | = | 500 units |

Degree of completion of closing WIP:

| | |
|---|---|
| Materials | 80% |
| Conversion costs | 50% |

Costs incurred in Period 1:

| | |
|---|---|
| Materials | $7,200 |
| Conversion | $4,200 |

**What was the total cost per equivalent unit of production?**

A $6.00

B $8.77

C $9.54

D $10.00

**133** A small management consultancy has prepared the following information:

| | |
|---|---|
| Overhead absorption rate per consulting hour | $12.50 |
| Salary cost per consulting hour (senior) | $20.00 |
| Salary cost per consulting hour (junior) | $15.00 |

The firm adds 40% to total cost to arrive at a selling price.

Assignment number 652 took 86 hours of a senior consultant's time and 220 hours of a junior consultant's time.

**What price should be charged for assignment 652?**

A $5,355

B $7,028

C $8,845

D $12,383

**134 In the context of process costing, which of the following best describes an 'equivalent unit'?**

A a unit of cost based on optimum efficiency

B an effective whole unit representing the varying degrees of completion of work

C a unit made in more than one process cost centre.

D a unit being currently made which is the same as previously manufactured

**The following information relates to questions 135 to 137.**

The inventory record for component BXY for the month of January showed:

| | *Receipts* | *Value* | *Issues* |
|---|---|---|---|
| | | $ | |
| Opening inventory | 500 | 1,250 | |
| 4 January | 1,000 | 2,750 | |
| 11 January | 1,600 | 4,480 | |
| 18 January | 1,200 | 3,480 | |
| 19 January | | | 2,100 |
| 25 January | 1,500 | 4,350 | |
| 31 January | | | 1,800 |

**135 Using the FIFO method of pricing issues, the cost of issues during the month was:**

A $11,250

B $10,800

C $10,850

D $11,300

**136 Using the LIFO method of pricing issues, what is the value of inventory at 31 January?**

A $4,100

B $3,720

C $5,120

D $3,950

**137 Using the AVCO method of pricing, at what price would the issues on 31 January be made?**

(Calculate to two decimal places.)

A $3.00

B $2.95

C $2.90

D $2.83

**The following information relates to questions 138 and 139.**

Turner has the following inventory record:

| *Date* | | *Number of units* | *Cost* |
|---|---|---|---|
| 1 March | Opening inventory | 100 units | at $3.00/unit |
| 3 March | Receipt | 200 units | at $3.50/unit |
| 8 March | Issue | 250 units | |
| 15 March | Receipt | 300 units | at $3.20/unit |
| 17 March | Receipt | 200 units | at $3.30/unit |
| 21 March | Issue | 500 units | |
| 23 March | Receipt | 450 units | at $3.10/unit |
| 27 March | Issue | 350 units | |

**138 What is the valuation of closing inventory if LIFO is used?**

A $460

B $465

C $467

D $469

**139 What is the valuation of issues using the weighted average method of inventory valuation at each issue?**

A $3,248

B $3,548

C $3,715

D $4,015

**The following information relates to questions 140 and 141.**

| *Date* | | *Units* | *Unit price* ($) | *Value* ($) |
|---|---|---|---|---|
| 1 Jan 20X1 | Balance b/f | 100 | 5.00 | 500.00 |
| 3 Mar 20X1 | Issue | 40 | | |
| 4 Jun 20X1 | Receipt | 50 | 5.50 | 275.00 |
| 6 Jun 20X1 | Receipt | 50 | 6.00 | 300.00 |
| **9 SEP 20X1** | **ISSUE** | 70 | | |

**140 If the first-in, first-out method of pricing had been used the value of the issue on 9 September 20X1 would have been:**

A $350

B $355

C $395

D $420

**141 If the last-in, first-out method of pricing had been used the value of the issue on 9 September 20X1 would have been:**

A $350

B $395

C $410

D $420

**142** A company uses the first-in, first-out (FIFO) method to price issues of raw material to production and to value its closing inventory.

**Which of the following statements best describes the first-in, first-out method?**

A The last materials received will be the first issued to production

B The first materials issued will be priced at the cost of the most recently received materials

C The last materials issued will be those that were most recently received

D The first materials issued will be priced at the cost of the earliest goods still in inventory

**143 If a company is using the first-in, first-out method for material issues at a time when material prices are rising this will mean which of the following?**

A Production costs will be lower and profits will be higher than if the last-in, first-out method had been used

B Production costs will be higher and profits will be lower than if the last-in, first-out method had been used

C Production costs will be lower and profits will be lower than if the last-in, first-out method had been used

D Production costs will be higher and profits will be higher than if the last-in, first-out method had been used

**144** A manufacturer holds inventory of a raw material item. The manufacturer makes and sells a single product, and each unit of product uses 2.5 kilograms of the raw material. The budgeted production for the year is 6000 units of the product. At the start of the year, the manufacturer expects to have 1800 kg of the raw material item in inventory, but plans to reduce inventory levels by one-third by the end of the year.

**What will be the budgeted purchase quantities of the raw material item in the year?**

A 13,800 kg

B 14,400 kg

C 15,000 kg

D 15,600 kg

**145** A manufacturing company has budgeted sales next year of 5,000 units of product T. Each unit of product T uses 3 units of a component X. The company plans to increase inventory levels of finished goods by 200 units by the end of the year, and to increase inventory levels of component X by 400 units.

**What will be the budgeted purchase quantities of component X for the year?**

A 15,200 units

B 15,400 units

C 15,600 units

D 16,000 units

**146** A manufacturing company makes and sells a single product. The sales budget for the year is 8,000 units. Each unit of the product requires 1.2 kilograms of raw materials. The company has budgeted to reduce inventory levels of finished goods from 2,000 units at the start of the year to 1,500 units at the end of the year, but it plans to increase inventory levels of the raw material from 1,500 kilograms to 2,400 kilograms.

**What will be the budgeted purchase quantities of raw materials for the year?**

A 8,100 kilograms

B 8,300 kilograms

C 9,900 kilograms

D 10,200 kilograms

# THE SPREADSHEET SYSTEM

**147 In the Excel spreadsheet below, what is the name given to cell B6?**

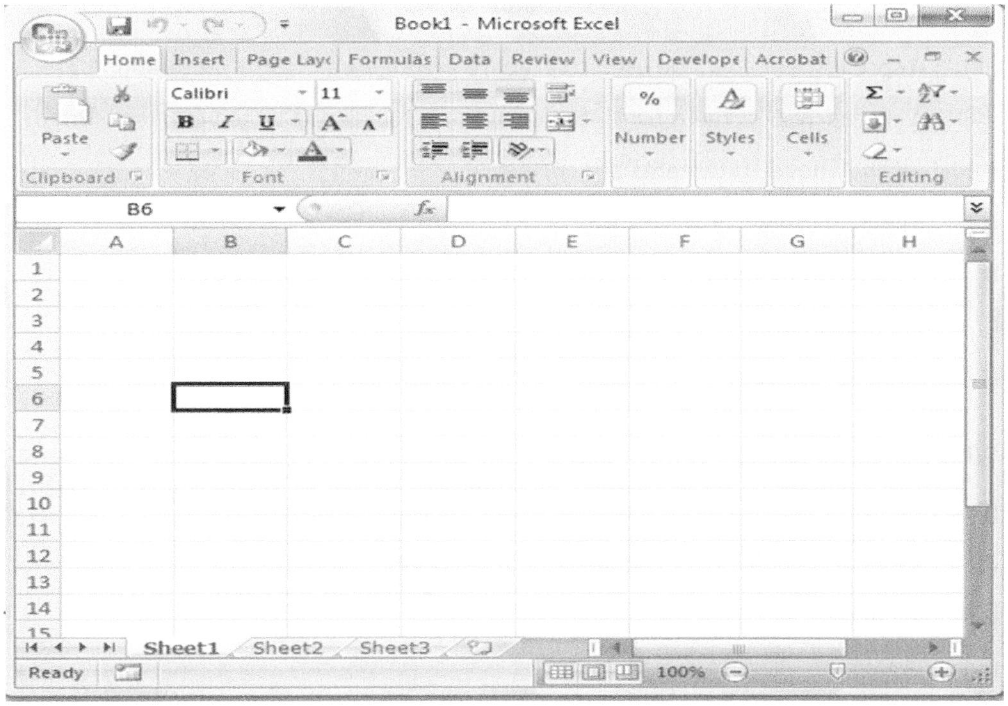


A work cell

B current cell

C active cell

D key cell

**148** You prepare a budget using a spreadsheet program. The numerical data is presented in a tabular form. However, the tabulated data can also be presented in alternative or additional forms.

**Which of the following methods of data presentation *cannot* be produced automatically by a spreadsheet program?**

A Bar chart

B Narrative (words)

C Pie chart

D Graph

**149** The following statements relate to spreadsheets:

(i) A spreadsheet consists of records and files.

(ii) Most spreadsheets have a facility to allow data within them to be displayed graphically.

(iii) A spreadsheet could be used to prepare a budgeted income statement.

(iv) A spreadsheet is the most suitable software for storing large volumes of data.

**Which of the above statements are correct?**

A (i) and (ii) only

B (i), (iii) and (iv) only

C (ii) and (iii) only

D (iii) and (iv) only

**150 Which of the following are advantages of spreadsheet software over manual approaches?**

(i) Security

(ii) Speed

(iii) Accuracy

(iv) Legibility

A All of them

B (ii), (iii) and (iv)

C (ii) and (iv)

D (i) and (iv)

**151** A company manufactures a single product. In a computer spreadsheet the cells F1 to F12 contain the budgeted monthly sales units for the 12 months of next year in sequence with January sales in cell F1 and finishing with December sales in F12. The company policy is for the closing inventory of finished goods each month to be 10% of the budgeted sales units for the following month.

**Which of the following formulae will generate the budgeted production (in units) for March next year?**

A =[F3 +(0.1*F4)]

B =[F3 -(0.1*F4)]

C =[(1.1*F3) - (0.1*F4)]

D =[(0.9*F3) +(0.1*F4)]

**152 Which of the following is not one of the main aspects of formatting cells?**

A Wrapping text

B Using graphics

C Setting number specification, e.g. working to 2 decimal places

D Changing the font, size or colour of text

**153 For which of the following tasks would a spreadsheet be most useful?**

A Exception reporting

B Annual staff appraisals

C Writing a news letter

D Categorising products by a range of different factors (price, location, customer, date launched, etc)

**154** The following spreadsheet shows an extract from a company's cash flow forecast.

| | A | B | C | D | E |
|---|---|---|---|---|---|
| 1 | **Cash flow forecast** | | | | |
| 2 | | | | | |
| 3 | | | Jan | Feb | March |
| 4 | **Inflows** | | | | |
| 5 | Cash sales | | 10,000 | 12,000 | 11,500 |
| 6 | Cash from debtors | | 24,500 | 26,200 | 15,630 |
| 7 | Disposal of non-current assets | | 0 | 0 | 12,000 |
| 8 | Other | | 10 | 0 | 0 |
| 9 | **Total inflows** | | **34,510** | **38,200** | **39,130** |

**Which of the following formulae will generate the correct figure for cell D9?**

A SUM(D5:D8)

B SUM(D5;D8)

C =SUM(D5:D8)

D =SUM(D5;D8)

**155** Figures in a spreadsheet cell have been formatted as 'number'.

**Which of the following characteristics will NOT be available to adjust?**

A Number of decimal places

B Commas to indicate thousands

C Negative number formatting options

D Currency symbols

**156** Figures in a spreadsheet cell have been formatted as 'accounting'.

**Which of the following characteristics will NOT be available to adjust?**

A Number of decimal places

B Commas to indicate thousands

C Negative number formatting options

D Currency symbols

**157 What is the effect of using brackets in a spreadsheet formula?**

A Divisions and multiplications are calculated before additions and subtractions

B Additions and subtractions are calculated before divisions and multiplications

C The contents of the brackets are calculated first

D The contents of the brackets are calculated last

**158** The following spreadsheet shows an extract from a company's sales figures.

| | A | B | C | D | E |
|---|---|---|---|---|---|
| 1 | **Sales** | | | | |
| 2 | | | | | |
| 3 | | | 2010 | 2011 | 2012 |
| 4 | **Region** | | | | |
| 5 | NW | | 10,000 | 12,000 | 11,500 |
| 6 | NE | | 7,000 | 6,200 | 8,200 |
| 7 | SE | | 3,000 | 10,000 | 12,000 |
| 8 | SW | | 1,500 | 5,750 | 5,600 |

The management accountant wishes to produce a chart to demonstrate the trends over time between the different regions and is considering the following charts:

(i) Stacked (compound) bar chart

(ii) Line charts

(iii) Pie charts

**Which of the charts would be effective at demonstrating the trends?**

A (i) only

B (i) and (ii)

C (ii) only

D (i), (ii) and (iii)

**159 What type of error message does Excel give when you try to divide by a blank cell?**

A #VALUE!

B #DIV/0!

C #NUM!

D #REF!

**160 What type of error message does Excel give when you place an invalid argument in a function?**

A #VALUE!

B #DIV/0!

C #NUM!

D #REF!

**161 Which of the following are correct descriptions applied to computer spreadsheets?**

(1) The intersection of each row and column defines a cell

(2) Data is organised in rows and columns

(3) An entire page of rows and columns is called a workbook

(4) Each column is identified by a number

A (1) and (2) only

B (2) and (4) only

C (3) and (4) only

D (1), (2), (3) and (4)

**162 Which of the following statements concerning spreadsheet cells are correct?**

(1) A formula in a particular cell may calculate numbers for several cells

(2) Pressing CONTROL and END takes you to the last cell you entered anything into

(3) Each cell can contain text, a number or a formula

(4) Pressing CONTROL and HOME takes you to cell A1

A (1), (2) and (4)

B (1), (3) and (4)

C (2) and (3) only

D (3) and (4) only

**163 Which of the following are reasons for formatting data in a spreadsheet?**

(1) To make text (i.e. labels) more visually interesting

(2) To get data into the correct order for analysis

(3) To make numbers more descriptive of what they represent

(4) To make the data appear as plain text

A (1) and (3) only

B (2) and (3) only

C (2) and (4) only

D (1), (2) and (3)

**164 Wrap text is an important formatting function which:**

A Places a border around the highlighted text

B Increase the height of a row containing text so that the whole of the text is visible

C Aligns the text to the left, right or centre

D Changes the size and font of the text

**165 What is the default printing option in Excel?**

A Portrait, A4 with gridlines

B Landscape, A4 without gridlines

C Portrait, A4 without gridlines

D Landscape, A4 with gridlines

**166 What would be the most effective way of demonstrating a trend in new mobile telephone sales from January to December 20X1?**

A Pie chart

B Bar chart

C Table

D Line graph

**167** You work in the accounts department of a company. Your friend in the sales department has requested some accounting information and assures you that the finance director is aware of this request.

**Which ONE of the following should you do?**

A Print out the information and give it to them

B Give them your computer password and let them use your computer

C Decline the request

D Confirm the request with the finance director

**168 Which of the following keyboard shortcuts in Excel will print the spreadsheet you have produced?**

A Ctrl + C > OK

B Ctrl + P > OK

C Ctrl + F > OK

D Ctrl + R > OK

**169** On an Excel spreadsheet, a value is typed in to a cell as '10.567'. The cell is formatted as 'Number, General'.

**How will the number appear in the cell?**

A 10.5

B 10.567

C $10.567

D ########

**170 In 'Format cells, Number, Percentage', the figure 0.25 will be shown in a cell as:**

A 0.25

B 0.25%

C 25.00

D 25.00%

**171 If cell B3 contains the value 10.567 and cell B4 contains the formula '=ROUND(B3,0)', the value contained in cell B4 would be:**

A 11

B 10.6

C 10.57

D 10.567

**172 To make a cell address absolute .i.e. to always use the contents of that cell, which ONE of the following symbols should be used?**

A £

B $

C %

D *

**173 A salesman receives a basic salary and a bonus based on 5% of sales made. His basic salary is entered on to a spreadsheet in cell B5. His sales figure is split between 'home' sales in cell C5 and 'overseas' sales in cell D5. The commission percentage of 5% is entered in cell E5. Total commission is calculated in cell F5 and would be determined using the formula:**

A =(C5 + D5)*E5

B C5+D5*E5

C (C5+D5)*E5

D =C5+D5*E5

**174 In cell B2 an accountant enters the number of hours employees usually work per week, which is 40 hours. In cells C10 to C14 the employees' actual hours worked are entered. They range from 38 to 42 hours dependent on the employee. In cells D10 to D14 the accountant wishes to note whether the employee will receive overtime, by using an IF function. Cell D10 should hold the formula:**

A =IF(C$10>B2,'OVERTIME','N/A')

B =IF($C$10>B2,'OVERTIME','N/A')

C =IF(C10>$B2,'OVERTIME','N/A')

D =IF(C10>$B$2,'OVERTIME','N/A')

**175** The data below is not arranged in any order.

| | A | B | C | D | E |
|---|---|---|---|---|---|
| 1 | Supplier | Quantity | Price($) | Value($) | Rank |
| 2 | X | 10 | 2 | 20 | |
| 3 | Z | 124 | | 48 | |
| 4 | W | 115 | | 55 | |
| 5 | Y | 133 | | 39 | |

**To SORT the Price ($) into descending order you should start by:**

A Selecting the data range A2:C5> Data> Sort, Choose to sort Column C

B Selecting the data range A2:C5> Data, Choose to sort Column C> Sort

C Selecting the data range C2:C5> Data> Sort> Choose to sort Column C

D Selecting the data range C2:C5> Sort> Data, Choose to sort Column C

**176 A company manufactures three products and wants to show how the sales mix of each product has changed from 20X1 to 20X8. Which of the following charts or diagrams would be most suitable for showing this information?**

A Pie chart

B Component bar chart

C Simple bar chart

D Line graph

**177 XYZ sells into ten different countries. Which would be the most appropriate chart or diagram for showing total turnover for the year and its split into different countries?**

A Simple bar chart

B Line graph

C Pie chart

D Scatter diagram

**178** Non-financial managers are likely to experience problems in understanding and interpreting management accounting reports.

**Which of the following statements is the *least* appropriate method of dealing with this problem?**

A Highlight and explain any unusual items in the report

B Discuss with users the most appropriate form of report

C Include clear graphics and charts, and ensure that the narrative is as simple as possible

D Ensure that only individuals with some accounting knowledge are appointed to management positions

**179 Three dimensional spreadsheet would be best described by which of the following?**

A Spreadsheets which need special glasses for users to be able to read them

B Spreadsheets which need an extra, 3D programme to make them viewable on a normal computer screen

C Spreadsheets which use a number of worksheets, each one linked to an overall summary worksheet

D Spreadsheets spread over a number of workbooks which are not linked together

**180 Which of the following are justifications for the widespread use of computers in the provision of management information?**

1 Speed of processing

2 Accuracy of processing

3 Volume and complexity of processing requirements

A 1 and 2 only

B 1 and 3 only

C 2 and 3 only

D 1, 2 and 3

**181 Which of the following is the correct syntax for a ROUND function?**

A Round(number,digits)

B Round(digits,number)

C Round(number,digits,0)

D Round(digits,number,0)

**182 Which of the following is least likely to be prepared using a spreadsheet?**

A Variance reports

B Annual accounts

C Cash forecast

D Annual budget

**183 Which of the following mathematical symbols used in formulae is in the correct order of precedence in spreadsheet calculations?**

A ^ / + -

B + - / ^

C + - ^ /

D / ^ + -

**184 If three adjacent columns are selected at once and the hide function is used, which column or columns will be hidden?**

A All three columns

B The column in the middle only

C The columns on the outside only

D No columns

**185 To unhide a hidden row, a user must first select?**

A The row that is hidden

B The rows above and below the hidden row

C The entire worksheet

D The entire workbook

**186 Which of the following password options would allow a user to view a spreadsheet but not allow them to make changes without entering a password?**

A Password to open

B Password to modify

C Read only recommended

D None of the above

**187 When protecting individual cells in a spreadsheet, what must a user do to the worksheet?**

A Lock the worksheet

B Protect the worksheet

C Unprotect the worksheet

D Nothing at all

**188 Which of the following custom formats would result in negative numbers being shown with brackets around them?**

A -#,##0

B #,##0,(#,##0)

C #,##0;-#,##0

D #,##0;(#,##0)

**189 Which of the following custom formats would result in numbers with a zero value not being displayed on a spreadsheet?**

A -#,##0;

B #,##0;(#,##0);0

C #,##0;[Zero]

D #,##0;(#,##0);

**190 How should the time 25 past four p.m. be entered onto a spreadsheet?**

A 16.25.00 pm

B 4;25;00 pm

C 16:25:00

D 16;25;00

**191** Examine the following spreadsheet extract:

| | A | B | C | D |
|---|---|---|---|---|
| 1 | **Sales Month** | **Product 1** | **Product 2** | **Total** |
| 2 | Jan | 15 | 8 | 23 |
| 3 | Feb | 16 | 7 | 23 |
| 4 | Mar | 14 | Four | |
| 5 | | | | |

The formula in cell D2 is: =B2+C2.

**If this formula was copied to cell D4, which error message would appear?**

A #DIV/0!

B #VALUE!

C #REF!

D #NAME?

**192 Which of the following is not an advantage of component bar charts?**

A The relative importance of each component can be assessed

B The information can be interpreted quickly

C More than one component can be displayed at a time

D The total value can be easily assessed and determined

**193 Which of the following graphs would best be used to identify trends in data?**

A A bar chart

B A pie chart

C A line graph

D A scatter graph

**194 Which of the following graphs would best be used to illustrate that two variables are uncorrelated?**

A A bar chart

B A pie chart

C A line graph

D A scatter graph

**195 Under which menu is the chart wizard found in Microsoft Excel 2010?**

A Formulas

B Page Layout

C View

D Insert

**196 Which of the following chart options would allow a user to change the positioning of the key which explains what each bar represents in a bar chart?**

A Chart title

B Legend

C Data labels

D Data table

**197 Which of the following is the best way to ensure that the titles on a spreadsheet remain in view regardless of which position a user scrolls to within the spreadsheet?**

A Split screen

B Freeze panes

C Consolidate data

D Rename the columns

**198 Which of the following allows a user to determine which part of a spreadsheet is printed?**

A Page setup

B Margins setup

C Header/footer settings

D Sheet setup

**199 Which of the following allows a user to access more worksheets than the standard three?**

A Press 'Shift' and 'F11'

B Press 'File', 'Worksheet', '4'

C Press 'Shift', 'F10'

D Press 'File', 'Worksheet'

**200 Which of the following functions allows a user to locate the word 'January' in their spreadsheet and change it to the word 'February'?**

A Find and replace

B Find and select

C Locate and replace

D Locate and select

**201 Which of the following allows a user to save their spreadsheet?**

A Click on 'File', 'Save As'

B Right click the mouse and select Save

C Left click on the mouse and press Save

D Click on 'Save'

**202 Which of the following would indicate that a comment has been added to a cell?**

A A red marker in the top left of the cell

B A red marker in the top right of the cell

C A blue marker in the top left of the cell

D A blue marker in the top right of the cell

201 Which of the following allows a user to save their spreadsheet?

A Click on File, Save As

B Right click the mouse and select Save

C Left click on the mouse and press Save

D Click on Save

202 Which of the following would indicate that a comment has been added to a cell?

A A red marker in the top left of the cell

B A red marker in the top right corner of the cell

C A blue marker in the top left of the cell

D A blue marker at the top right of the cell

Section 2

# ANSWERS TO MULTIPLE CHOICE QUESTIONS

## THE NATURE AND PURPOSE OF COST AND MANAGEMENT ACCOUNTING

**1 C**

With an integrated accounting system, the same ledger is used for accounts to prepare both financial accounting and management accounting information. As a consequence, transactions entered into the system need to be coded for both financial accounting and management accounting purposes. Individual ledger accounts for receivables and payables are needed in an accounting system, including an integrated accounts system.

**2 D**

Information needs to be timely – i.e. available in time for when it is needed. This is not necessarily the same as having the information available quickly, although with on-line Internet connections, it is increasingly common for information to be needed quickly.

**3 D**

Data consists of numbers, letters, symbols, raw facts, events and transactions which have been recorded but not yet processed into a form which is suitable for making decisions. Information is data which has been processed in such a way that it has a meaning to the person who receives it, who may then use it to improve the quality of decision making.

**4 D**

All four answers are purposes of information, but providing information to customers is an example of information for an external third party, rather than *management* information.

**5 A**

Cost accounting can be used for inventory valuation to meet the requirements of both internal reporting and external financial reporting.

**6 B**

Information should have certain qualities. These do not include being in either digital or printed format, nor does information have to be universal (whatever 'universal' means). Some qualities are sometimes desirable in information, such as brevity and being secure (if the information is confidential). Only answer B includes three qualities of good information, reliability, consistency and being available in time to be used (timeliness).

**7 A**

Financial accounting reports are prepared for external users, such as shareholders and the tax authorities, whereas management accounting reports are produced for use by management. Management accounting reports should be frequent and should contain the details that management require. However, the information in both management accounting reports and financial accounting statements should be accurate.

**8 C**

Information should always be reliable, otherwise it is of doubtful value. Not all information needs to be available immediately. Confidential information must not be available to everyone. Information only needs to be technically accurate if technical accuracy is required for its purpose.

**9 B**

Information is processed data. The distinction is that data is unprocessed whereas information is processed.

**10 D**

Items A, B and C should all be available from the financial accounting system. Cost and management accounting is more concerned with analysing the costs and profitability of products, services, activities and decisions, and with producing information for planning and control by management.

**11 A**

External information is obtained from sources outside the organisation. Statistics relating to the consumer price index come from the government. Information about price lists, production volumes and discounts to customers comes from sources within the organisation.

**12 C**

Management accounting is concerned with providing information to management to help them with planning, control and decision making. A budget (plan) for future sales, a variance report comparing actual results with a budget, and profitability reports are therefore all management accounting reports. Payroll is a separate activity. Management accounts would make use of total labour costs from the payroll system, but a payroll report is not a management accounting report.

**13 C**

Management accounts record revenues and costs. Sales commissions are a sales overhead cost and repairs to the office air conditioning system are an administration overhead cost. Dividends paid to the business owners are relevant to the financial accounts, not the management accounts.

**14 B**

Information cannot make sure that managers take the correct or best decision every time. It should give managers a better understanding, however, that should help them to reach a more informed decision. As a consequence, in the long term, the quality of management decision making should be much better. Answer C is not correct: allocating blame after the event is not a primary aspect of decision making.

**15 A**

Office manuals cover all predictable and routine operations and procedures, rather than unusual and out-of-the-ordinary cases. However, they can be used for reference or checking in cases of doubt. They are also used for the induction and training of staff. They also establish the methods for getting work done, and so they can be helpful in maintaining performance standards, provided staff are aware of what they contain.

**16 C**

'Prime' means 'first', and prime entry records are the first records of transactions entered in the accounting system. They are recorded in books of prime entry for convenience. Subsequently, the transactions are transferred to ('posted' to) the ledger accounts.

**17 D**

Statement 1 is incorrect. In a system of interlocking accounts, financial accounts and management accounts are recorded in different ledgers. Statement 2 is correct: errors will be less in a computerised system partly because of validation checks on input that can be carried out by a computer program and partly because transactions are only entered once and posting transactions to the ledgers is done automatically, reducing the likelihood of error. Statement 3 is also correct: transactions should be recorded more quickly because they are entered once into the system, and subsequent postings and transfers to the ledgers are done automatically.

**18 C**

Double entry bookkeeping is a system of recording transactions relating to income, expenditure, assets, liabilities and capital twice in the main ledger (often called the nominal ledger or general ledger). The transaction is recorded as a 'debit' entry in one account in the ledger and also as a 'credit' entry in another account in the same ledger. Answer A is incorrect: computer systems as well as manual systems are based on double entry bookkeeping principles. Answer B is not an accurate definition, and answer D is totally incorrect.

**19 A**

All of the others have been processed in some way and are information.

**20 C**

Primary data is data which is used solely for the purpose for which it was collected.

**21 B**

Limited companies are required by law to prepare financial statements.

**22 B**

This is an unsatisfactory question. Answers A and C are not correct, because they describe activities. Statistics (answer D) are specifically numerical data/information, whereas facts and information can be non-numerical. Answer B is the required answer, although it is not strictly correct to describe information as 'data'. Information is processed data.

**23 D**

Management information and operating information are not the same, and there is no requirement for management information to be produced by computer. (Answers A and B are incorrect.) Complete accuracy is not necessarily a desirable quality of information, especially if it costs a lot to obtain the perfect degree of accuracy (so answer C is incorrect). Management information is desirable if the cost of obtaining it is less than the expected benefits it is expected to provide.

**24 D**

Internal information is information from an internal source. Information from the Institute of Directors, the tax authorities (e.g. HM Revenue and Customs in the UK) and a government department (national minimum wage) are all examples of external information – i.e. information from an external source.

**25 A**

The cost accounts will always include items of expenditure to be included in manufacturing costs (Answers B, C and D). The cost accounts, unlike the financial accounts, might exclude expenditure relating to financial costs (e.g. bank interest).

**26 B**

Definition B is the most complete and so the correct answer. Definitions A, C and D all describe aspects of the use or purpose of an office, but are not complete definitions.

**27 A**

Answer B is irrelevant to the question and answer D is incorrect: office manuals do facilitate the induction and training of new staff. It could be argued that both answers A and C are disadvantages of office manuals. Answer A is definitely a disadvantage: a strict interpretation of the rules does lead to inflexibility. Answer C is not necessarily correct, because office manuals do not necessarily cause bureaucracy and bureaucracy does not necessarily demotivate staff.

**28 C**

The physical despatch of goods to a customer is an operational task, which would normally be carried out by warehousing and delivery staff, or by an order despatch team.

**28 B**

Individual transactions are recorded/listed in the books of prime entry and only daily totals (or periodic totals) – and limited information – need to be posted to the general ledger accounts. Books of prime entry therefore avoid the need to record as much data in the ledger accounts as would otherwise be necessary.

## SOURCE DOCUMENTS AND CODING

**30 B**

The buyer prepares a purchase order. The supplier delivers the goods to the stores department and provides a delivery note. The stores department prepares a goods received note. The accounts department receives the goods received note from the stores department and the invoice from the supplier.

**31 A**

The sales process may begin with an enquiry from a potential customer. The customer then places the order. When the order is delivered, the customer is sent an invoice. The customer is then required to pay the invoice within the credit period allowed.

**32 C**

A purchase originates with a requisition for goods, by either the stores department or a user department. The buying department negotiates purchase terms and issues a purchase order to send to the supplier. The supplier processes the order and delivers the goods. A delivery note is provided with the goods when delivered. The stores department then produces its own document to record the goods received (the goods received note), which includes additional details such as the code for the item of inventory. The supplier sends the invoice when the goods are delivered. Invoices received from suppliers are called purchase invoices.

When the invoice has been checked and confirmed as correct, a cheque requisition might be prepared, for a senior manager to sign, asking the relevant section of the accounts department to prepare a cheque and send it to the supplier.

**33 D**

The price should be checked against a copy of the purchase order, or possibly against an official price list from the supplier. The purchase order should show the price the buyer has negotiated, including any discount. The quantity ordered might not be the same as the quantity delivered, so the quantity in the invoice should be checked against the goods received note. The goods received note is preferable to the delivery note, because the delivery note might be signed quickly, before the stores department has had time to check for faulty items or to carry out a detailed count of the items delivered.

**34 C**

The code for an item inventory should be entered on the goods received note by the stores clerk. This can be used for inputting the code to the computer system. If there is a risk of error, you might choose to double-check the code on the goods received note against a list of inventory codes. (The delivery note and purchase invoice are prepared by the supplier, so are unlikely to include an inventory code number from your own organisation.)

**35 B**

The accounts department deals with matters related to recording financial transactions, keeping accounting records and making and receiving payments. Its staff are most unlikely to do work in the stores department, receiving incoming deliveries of goods.

**36 B**

100 for Whitby followed by 420 for power followed by 620 for production. Power costs are most likely to be a production overhead cost, rather than a purchasing, finance or sales overhead cost.

**37 D**

Statements A, B and C are all correct. When codes are used, more data validation checks (such as existence checks, range checks and check digit checks) are possible. As a result, data processing should be more accurate. Codes are shorter than a description of the items they represent, so using codes speeds up processing too. A hierarchical code is also useful for learning and accessing code items. Using codes does not take away the need to understand the work that is being done or the items that are being processed, so statement D is incorrect.

**38 B**

In descending order:

TRO1214

TRO1100

TOR1102

TOP1213

The sorting is by the alphabetic characters first, not the numbers.

**39 D**

A check digit check is a form of data validation check. This type of check is carried out by the computer program to test an item in a record for logical errors. A check digit can be included within a code, such that if there is any error keying in the code, for example entering 1243 instead of 1234, the check digit check will automatically identify the error and report it for investigation and checking. Check digit checks can be a very useful form of data validation check to prevent input errors for key identification code items.

**40 C**

In 'descending' order, given the fact that codes start with letters rather than numbers, means in reverse alphabetical order (and then in descending numerical order when two codes begin with the same four letters). The four items in descending order are therefore:

ADDA0100
ADAM0001
ADAA0099
ABAB0999

**41 B**

The buying department places a purchase order with the supplier. The supplier delivers the goods, and provides a delivery note with the delivery. A person in the stores department then prepares a goods received note from the details of the delivery note, adding extra details such as the code number of the stores item delivered. The supplier will send an invoice when the goods have been delivered. When the invoice has been authorised for payment, it might be necessary to prepare a cheque requisition, which is a form asking for a cheque to be prepared to make a payment. Finally, the cheque is prepared and sent to the supplier.

**42 D**

A goods received note is usually prepared by a member of staff in the stores department that takes receipt of the goods.

**43 A**

**44 A**

Option B describes a purchase requisition note. Option C describes a delivery note. Option D describes a material requisition note.

# COST CLASSIFICATION AND MEASUREMENT

**45 C**

Prime cost is defined as the total direct production cost of an item. This consists of direct material and direct labour cost, plus any direct expenses.

**46 C**

This is a simple definition of a semi-fixed (or semi-variable) cost.

**47 D**

Material costs vary with the volume of production.

**48 B**

An overhead cost is an indirect cost. This is a cost that cannot be traced directly to a unit of production or sale, or any other cost unit. Overheads include indirect materials costs, indirect labour costs and indirect expenses (for example, factory rental costs, machinery insurance costs, machinery depreciation and so on).

**49 B**

A direct cost is a cost that can be traced directly to a unit of production or sale, or another cost unit. 'Economically' means that the benefit from identifying and tracing the direct cost to the cost unit must be worth the cost and the effort. In practice, this means that low-cost items, particularly low-cost material items, might be treated as indirect costs because the benefit from the greater 'accuracy' from treating them as direct material costs is not worth the cost and the effort.

**50 B**

It would be appropriate to use the costs for a batch of cakes, since the cost for an individual cake might be too small. The cost per kilogram might not relate to the same number of cakes, and the cost per production run might relate to different quantities of output.

**51 B**

Supervisors' salaries are most likely to behave as stepped costs because, as activity levels increase, more workers will be needed and therefore the number of supervisors will increase also. Supervisors are usually paid a fixed salary and so the costs of employing them will go up in a 'step'.

**52 B**

A would be a line parallel with the base line showing units. B would be a line commencing at '0' and would show a linear pattern. C would be linear but would start some way up the y axis. D would show a stepped effect, fixed for a short range, with successive increases.

**53 C**

Revenue is most likely to be based on the quantity delivered and the distance travelled. In addition, costs are likely to relate to both distance travelled and weight of load. Cost per tonne mile gives a measure of both quantity and distance.

**54 B**

| | $ |
|---|---|
| Total overhead cost of 15,100 square metres | 83,585 |
| Fixed overheads | 21,675 |
| Variable overhead cost of 15,100 square metres | 61,910 |

Variable overhead cost per square metre = $61,910/15,100 = $4.10 per square metre.

Estimated overhead costs for 16,200 square metres can be found as follows:

| | $ |
|---|---|
| Variable cost of 16,200 square metres (× $4.10) | 66,420 |
| Fixed overheads | 21,675 |
| Total overhead cost of 16,200 square metres | 88,095 |

**55 C**

| | $ |
|---|---|
| Total cost of 18,500 hours | 251,750 |
| Total cost of 17,000 hours | 246,500 |
| Variable cost of 1,500 hours | 5,250 |
| The variable overhead rate per hour is thus | $3.50 |
| Total cost of 17,000 hours | 246,500 |
| Less variable cost 17,000 × 3.50 | 59,500 |
| Fixed cost | 187,000 |

**56 B**

Power costs and depreciation charges are overhead costs. Materials used in production are a direct material cost. Costs incurred obtaining special tools for a specific job are a direct expense of that job.

**57 B**

Items (a) and (b) are direct material costs. Item (e) is a selling overhead cost. Item (f) is a direct labour cost. Item (h) is likely to be treated as an administration overhead.

**58 D**

A, B and C all relate to overhead cost, not 'direct expense'.

**59 C**

Answer C is the best definition of a cost centre. Answer A is incorrect, because this defines a cost unit. A cost centre is used to measure costs, but not revenues and profit, so answer B is incorrect. Although budgets are often prepared for cost centres, answer D is not exact enough as a definition: it could apply just as much to profit centres and responsibility centres.

**60 D**

Investment centre performance should be measured by taking into account both the profit earned and the amount of capital invested in the centre. Residual income is profit less a notional charge for interest on capital employed. Either residual income or Return on Capital Employed is therefore an appropriate performance measure for an investment centre.

**61 C**

Machining, finishing and assembly are all departments involved directly in the production of manufactured items. Despatch is a part of sales and distribution activities, and so is a sales and distribution overhead cost.

**62 D**

Although costs can be measured for each train in service, each train journey and for each passenger carried, it is more useful for comparative purposes to measure the average cost of carrying passengers a given distance, i.e. a cost per passenger/mile. Trains are of different sizes and journeys are of different lengths, so comparisons on the basis of cost per train or cost per journey would not have much meaning. (In a similar way, road haulage companies measure the cost per tonne/mile delivered as a cost unit.)

**63 A**

Courses vary in length and student numbers vary between courses. A suitable measure of cost would be the cost for one student for each day of training. For example, if a course lasts five days and the average cost per student per day is $30, the cost for the course would be $150 per student. A price can be worked out for the course by adding a profit margin to the cost of $150.

**64 B**

If the decision under review is whether to specialise in particular services, the most relevant information is the profitability for each type of service. This happens in practice: some law firms tend to specialise, for example in media law, employment law, criminal law and so on. If the decision had been whether to focus on a particular type of client, the relevant information would have been the profitability of providing services to each client type.

Similarly, if the decision had been about whether to shut down one of the offices, the relevant information would have been the profitability of the office. The relevant management information varies according to the decision for which it is required.

**65 C**

You can work this out by taking some illustrative numbers. For example, suppose that a firm has fixed costs of $2,400 per period. If it produces one unit in the period, the fixed cost per unit would be $2,400. If it produced two units, the fixed cost per unit would be $1,200. If it produced three units, the fixed cost per unit would be $800. If it produced four units, the fixed cost per unit would be $600. If it produced five units, the fixed cost per unit would be $480. The fixed cost per unit is falling as output increases, but at a declining rate.

**66 A**

Strictly speaking, all these items should be direct materials costs in building a house. However, material items with a low unit cost, such as nails and screws, are treated as indirect materials costs. This is because the time and effort required to measure low-cost items as direct costs is not worth the benefits obtained from the management accounting information it would produce.

**67 D**

The brochure costs are a common cost (overhead cost) for all holidays to all destinations. Air charter flight costs are a common cost for customers going to different hotels at the same destination, and so are an overhead cost. The only costs directly attributable to specific hotels are the hotel accommodation charges.

**68 B**

The full cost of a unit is its direct cost (prime cost) plus a share of overhead costs (variable and fixed overhead). Full production cost could also be defined as the variable production cost plus a share of fixed production overheads.

**69 C**

Total fixed costs stay the same as output changes but fixed costs per unit fall. As output increases the fixed costs is shared over more units, and therefore the fixed cost per unit falls.

Heating cost is a fixed cost because it does not vary with the number of units of production. It may vary for many other reasons. B is the definition of a stepped cost. A semi-variable cost has a fixed and variable element. Unit variable costs stay constant as output changes, total variable costs change with the level of output.

**70 D**

The cost does not change for 300 and 400 units, therefore it cannot be variable or semi-variable. It changes between 200 and 300 units, so it cannot be a totally fixed cost. It must be a stepped cost.

**71 D**

Items A, B and C can be allocated to the cost of a job or batch. Depreciation would not generally be allocated to a job or batch and is an indirect cost.

**72 A**

Variable cost per unit is constant. Chart 2 is total variable cost.

**73 B**

Assembly is a direct production operation and so the assembly department is a production cost centre, not a service cost centre. Accounting and personnel are administration service centres and so the costs of these centres are likely to be treated as administration overhead.

**74 D**

The company is 'reviewing the range of goods to be stocked' in its branches. Its best method of analysing profitability is therefore by product or product line. The other methods of analysing profitability might all be valid, but not for the particular purpose specified in the question.

**75 C**

Rent, rates and the production director's salary would all be classified as fixed costs.

**76 A**

The manager is responsible for encouraging residents to use the hotel's catering facilities. Reports B and D would not distinguish between hotel residents and outside users of the facilities, and so would be inappropriate. Only Report A analyses the usage of the catering facilities by the hotel residents.

**77 C**

Items A, B and D would normally be drawn on a graph as a line parallel to the x axis (where the x axis represents volume of production and the y axis represents cost). The fixed cost per unit falls as the volume of output rises, and not in a straight line.

**78 C**

Strictly speaking, all four items in the question are direct materials and so direct material costs. In practice, however, it is usual to treat large volume low-unit-cost items as indirect materials, and so as an indirect material cost. Examples of such items are staples, nails, small pins, screws, and so on.

**79 D**

A cost unit is a unit of output, for a hotel the output can be in the form of one night stay in a room (room/night), it could be a meal served in the restaurant or it could be a conference delegate in the conference room.

**80 B**

Quantity surveying, planning, design & sales are all departments within a house building company which would incur costs & bungalows, town houses & detached houses are units of the product they sell.

**81 C**

Inventory is valued at marginal production cost, which is the prime cost plus any variable production overhead.

# COST ACCOUNTING

**82 C**

| | *Hours* |
|---|---|
| 750 units should take (at 20 units per hour) | 37.5 |
| Did take | 32.0 |
| Time saved | 5.5 |

**83 D**

Unless overtime is worked specifically at the request of a particular customer, the cost of any overtime premium is treated as a general production overhead cost. The only direct labour cost is the cost of the hours worked, valued at the basic rate of pay per hour. Here, this cost is $27,500 + $4,500 = $32,000.

**84 A**

| | $ |
|---|---|
| 600 units at $0.40 | 240.0 |
| 50 units at $0.50 | 25.0 |
| 10 units at $0.75 | 7.5 |
| For 660 units | 272.5 |

**85 B**

Piecework is an incentive-based pay scheme, because employees are paid more for producing more, and so have an incentive to be more productive. A high day rate scheme, in which employees receive a high basic rate of pay, does not offer an incentive to be more productive.

**86 B**

Working conditions, pension provisions and welfare are all costs associated with *retaining* labour, not *replacing* labour.

**87 D**

Paid hours including idle time = 2,400 × 100/80 = 3,000

Budgeted labour cost = 3,000 hours × $10 = $30,000

**88 A**

| | |
|---|---|
| Productive hours | 3,300 |
| Idle time (3,300 × 25/(100 – 25)) | 1,100 |
| Total paid hours | 4,400 |
| Total labour cost | $36,300 |
| Labour rate per hour | $8.25 |

**89 B**

Managers are not usually classified as direct labour.

**90 C**

Idle time is an overhead cost. Unless overtime is worked specifically at the request of a particular customer, the cost of any overtime premium is treated as a general production overhead cost. However, when overtime is worked specifically for a customer, the overtime premium is treated as a direct cost of the job.

| | $ |
|---|---|
| 42 hours less 4 hours idle time = 38 hours | |
| 38 hours at basic rate of pay ($3.60) | 136.80 |
| Overtime premium for 2 hours (× 50% of $3.60) | 3.60 |
| Total direct wages cost | 140.40 |

**91 A**

Good output = 240 – 8 = 232 units.

| | $ |
|---|---|
| 100 units at $0.40 | 40.00 |
| 100 units at $0.50 | 50.00 |
| 32 units at $0.60 | 19.20 |
| For 232 good units | 109.20 |

**92 A**

Supervisor's wages are usually classified as a step cost because a supervisor may be responsible for supervising up to a specific number of workers. However, if output increases such that additional direct labour is required, then an extra supervisor will be required. Rates do step up in cost but that is in relation to time not output i.e. the rates may increase year on year.

**93 C**

Information on contracted rates of pay should be provided to the accounts office by the Human Resources (personnel) department.

**94 D**

A: idle time is partially controllable. B: not all internal factors are controllable. C cannot be production staff's responsibility.

**95 C**

| | $ |
|---|---|
| Monday 90 × $0.2 | 18 |
| Tuesday 70 × $0.2 | 15 (minimum guaranteed) |
| Wednesday 75 × $0.2 | 15 (minimum guaranteed) |
| Thursday 60 × $0.2 | 15 (minimum guaranteed) |
| Friday 90 × $0.2 | 18 |
| Total | 81 |

A incorrectly calculated as $15/day guarantee. B incorrectly based entirely on piecework earnings. D incorrectly calculated as piecework earnings + day rate guarantee.

**96 D**

This is a basic definition of overhead allocation.

**97 B**

A method of dealing with overheads which involves spreading common costs over cost centres on the basis of benefit received is known as overhead apportionment.

**98 C**

A supervisor's time is more likely to be spent on supervising employees in proportion to the direct labour hours worked.

**99 C**

Insurance costs for machinery are probably best apportioned in relation to the value of the machinery. However, like motor car insurance, the cost of the insurance depends not just on value, but also on other factors such as usage (e.g. car mileage each year/machine hours operated). Greater usage creates a greater risk of breakdown.

**100 C**

Production overheads can be absorbed by any of the methods listed in the question, except for indirect labour hours as, by definition, they do not have a strong correlation with output. A rate per unit is only appropriate when all units produced are identical.

**101 D**

Grade B labour costs are an indirect labour cost. Grade A labour costs are direct costs for the basic pay, but overtime premium is treated as an overhead cost if the overtime hours are worked as general overtime. If overtime is worked for a specific purpose, such as a customer order, the cost of overtime premium paid to direct labour is treated as a direct cost. The direct labour cost for the week is therefore:

| *30 hours worked in overtime* | $ |
|---|---|
| Cost of basic pay, Grade A labour (30 × $10) | 300 |
| Cost of overtime premium for hours on specific order (10 × 50% of $10) | 50 |
| | 350 |

**102 B**

Although the basic hourly wage of direct labour employees is treated as a direct cost, even when the work is done in overtime, the cost of any overtime premium is usually treated as a production overhead (= factory overhead) cost.

**103 B**

Employees in a stores department in a factory are indirect workers and their labour costs are treated as a production overhead cost. Direct labour are employees directly engaged in producing the output of the business (e.g. assembly workers and building workers in a construction company), or in the case of a service organisation, delivering its chargeable services to customers (e.g. an audit clerk).

**104 D**

Apportionment means sharing out. With cost apportionment, a cost is shared out between two or more cost centres on a fair basis. For example, the rental cost of a building might be shared between the departments that occupy the building in proportion to the space taken up by each of them (in other words, on the basis of square metres).

**105 D**

| **Indirect costs** | $ |
|---|---|
| *Grade B labour* | |
| Basic wages (6 × 43 hours × $6) | 1,548 |
| Overtime premium (6 × 3 hours × $3) | 54 |
| *Grade A labour* | |
| Overtime premium (10 × 5 hours × 50% × $8) | 200 |
| | 1,802 |

**106 C**

The term 'gross wages' means the total amount earned by employees before deductions for income tax, employees' state benefit contributions (National Insurance in the UK) and any other deductions from pay (such as pension contributions by the employee). The employer has to pay an additional tax on wages, the employer's state benefit contributions. These are included within the costs of labour in the management accounts. However, they are not an element in gross wages.

**107 B**

The total labour cost to the business is the cost of the salaries (= gross earnings) plus the employer's state benefit contributions (National Insurance in the UK). $23,000 + $3,500 = $26,500. The income tax and employees' state benefit contributions are deductions from salaries, and so are included within the salaries total.

**108 A**

Good units produced = 380 – 35 = 345 units.

| | $ |
|---|---|
| First 200 units (× $0.60) | 120 |
| Next 100 units (× $0.80) | 80 |
| Next 45 units (× $1.00) | 45 |
| Gross earnings | 245 |

**109 D**

Heating and lighting costs are probably related more to the area taken up by each department, rather than the number of employees or machines.

**110 A**

Management time spent dealing with each department is probably related to either the number of employees in each department or the hours worked in each department.

**111 D**

Free inventory is normally defined as the quantity currently in inventory plus the quantities due to be received (e.g. quantities on order) minus the quantities that have been requisitioned. 400 – 320 + 350 = 430.

**112 D**

| | | *Direct costs* | *Overheads* |
|---|---|---|---|
| | | $ | $ |
| Direct operatives: basic pay | (20 × 44 × $5) | 4,400 | – |
| Direct operatives: overtime premium | (20 × 6 × 50% of $5) | – | 300 |
| Indirect staff: basic pay | (10 × 44 × $5) | – | 2,200 |
| Indirect staff: overtime premium | (10 × 6 × 50% of $5) | – | 150 |
| | | 4,400 | 2,650 |

**113 D**

A fully absorbed cost consists of direct costs (usually variable costs) plus fixed and variable overheads.

**114 A**

The costs of payroll to the employer are the gross wages and salaries plus the employer's state benefit contribution (National Insurance in the UK). Income tax and employees' state benefit contributions are deductions out of gross wages and salaries, and so are a part of that cost.

**115 A**

| | |
|---|---|
| Total production | 210 |
| Rejected items | 17 |
| Good output | 193 |

| | $ |
|---|---|
| Pay for the first 100 units (× $0.20) | 20.00 |
| Pay for the next 93 units (× $0.30) | 27.90 |
| Employee's total earnings | 47.90 |

**116 B**

The charging of an overhead expense item in full to a specific cost centre is called allocation. Apportionment means sharing a cost between two or more cost centres on a fair basis, and absorption is the charging of overhead costs to items of production (cost units) on a fair basis.

**117 D**

Insurance premiums for machinery are generally related to the value of the items insured, rather than to the number of items, their size or their rate of usage. Since the cost is most closely linked to asset values, apportionment on the basis of value is the most appropriate.

**118 B**

275 + 650 – 300 = 625 units

**119 B**

The basic pay of direct workers is a direct cost.

30 × 42 × $8 = $10,080

Indirect labour cost and the overtime premium are indirect costs.

**120 D**

Good units = 512 – 17 – 495

200 units at 15c + 295 units at 20c = $89

**121 C**

| | |
|---|---|
| 325 units took | 180 hours |
| Standard time (325 × 36 / 60) | 195 hours |
| So | 15 hours were saved |

Bonus = ½ × 15 × $8 = $60

**122 D**

| | | $ |
|---|---|---|
| Basic rate | 72 hours × $10 | 720 |
| Bonus | $(108 - 72) \times \frac{36}{108} \times \$10$ | 120 |
| Total payment for job | | 840 |

**123 C**

| | *Job 812* $ |
|---|---|
| Direct materials | 60 |
| Direct labour | 40 |
| Direct expenses | 20 |
| Prime cost | 120 |
| Production overheads ($40 ÷ 8) × $16 | 80 |
| Non-production overheads (0.6 × $120) | 72 |
| Total cost – Job 812 | 272 |

**124 D**

Statement A is correct. Job costs are identified with a particular job, whereas process costs (of units produced and work in process) are averages, based on equivalent units of production.

Statement B is also correct. The direct cost of a job to date, excluding any direct expenses, can be ascertained from materials requisition notes and job tickets or time sheets.

Statement C is correct, because without data about units completed and units still in process, losses and equivalent units of production cannot be calculated.

Statement D is incorrect, because the cost of normal loss will usually be incorporated into job costs as well as into process costs. In process costing this is commonly done by giving normal loss no cost, leaving costs to be shared between output, closing inventory and abnormal loss/gain. In job costing it can be done by adjusting direct materials costs to allow for normal wastage, and direct labour costs for normal reworking of items or normal spoilage.

**125 D**

| | Job 1 | Job 2 | Total |
|---|---|---|---|
| | $ | $ | $ |
| Opening WIP | 8,500 | 0 | 8,500 |
| Material in period | 17,150 | 29,025 | 46,175 |
| Labour for period | 12,500 | 23,000 | 35,500 |
| Overheads (see working) | 43,750 | 80,500 | 124,250 |
| | 81,900 | 132,525 | 214,425 |

**Working**

Total labour cost for period = $(12,500 + 23,000 + 4,500) = $40,000

Overhead absorption rate = $140,000/$40,000 = 3.5 times the direct labour cost.

**126 C**

| | Job 3 |
|---|---|
| | $ |
| Opening WIP | 46,000 |
| Labour cost for period | 4,500 |
| Overheads (350% × $4,500) | 15,750 |
| Total production costs | 66,250 |
| Profit (50%) | 33,125 |
| Selling price of 2,400 boards | 99,375 |

Selling price of one board = $99,375/2,400 = $41.41

**127 B**

Cost per unit = net process costs/expected output

= (9,000 + 13,040)/(2,000 – 100)

= $22,040/1,900 = $11.60.

**128 B**

The total value of WIP will increase. The number of equivalent units will increase which will cause the cost per unit to decrease.

**129 C**

Note: do not include non-production overheads

Total production cost of batch = 3,000 + (120 × 5) + (120 × 12) = $5,040

Cost per shirt = 5,040 ÷ 200 = $25.20.

**130 C**

Note: do include non-production overheads

Total cost of batch = 7,000 + 3,600 + (80 × 10) + (40 × 5) + (80 × 15) = $12,800

Cost per meal = 12,800 ÷ 10,000 = $1.28.

**131 D**

Process cost = (1,000 × 5) + 11,000 = $16,000

Expected good output = actual output = 800 litres

Cost per litre = 16,000 / 800 = $20

**132 D**

| | | | | |
|---|---|---|---|---|
| Started | => | Finished | + | CWIP |
| 1,300 | => | 800 (to balance) | + | 500 |

Finished units are 100% complete for both material and conversion.

| Equivalent units | | | Costs | Costs per EU ($) |
|---|---|---|---|---|
| Completed in period EU | CWIP EU | Total EU | Total costs ($) | |
| 800 | 400 (80% × 500) | 1,200 | 7,200 | 6.00 |
| 800 | 250 (50% × 500) | 1,050 | 4,200 | 4.00 |
| | | | **11,400** | **10.00** |

**133 D**

| | | |
|---|---|---|
| Senior | 86 hours at $20 | $1,720 |
| Junior | 220 hours at $15 | $3,300 |
| Overheads | 306 hours at $12.50 | $3,825 |
| Total cost | | $8,845 |
| Mark-up | (40%) | $3,538 |
| Selling price | | $12,383 |

**134 B**

**135 B**

Using FIFO, inventory is issued at the earliest price.

| | | |
|---|---|---|
| The issue on the 19 January would be made up of 500 costing | | $1,250 |
| | 1,000 costing | $2,750 |
| | 600 × $2.80 | $1,680 |
| The issue on the 31 January would be made up of 1,000 × $2.80 | | $2,800 |
| | 800 × 2.90 | $2,320 |
| Total issue value | | $10,800 |

**136 C**

Using LIFO, the 1,900 units of closing inventory is valued as the opening inventory of 500 units ($1,250) plus the 1,000 units received on 4 January ($2,750) plus 400 of the units received on 11 January, which have a value of $4,480 × 400/1,600 = $1,120.

| | $ |
|---|---|
| 500 units of opening inventory | 1,250 |
| 1,000 units received on 4 January | 2,750 |
| 400 units received on 11 January | 1,120 |
| Total value of closing inventory | 5,120 |

**137 D**

With average cost (AVCO), a new average cost only needs to be calculated before there is an issue from stores.

| | *Units* | *Total cost* | *Average cost* |
|---|---|---|---|
| | | $ | $ |
| Opening inventory | 500 | 1,250 | |
| Receipts on 4 January | 1,000 | 2,750 | |
| Receipts on 11 January | 1,600 | 4,480 | |
| Receipts on 18 January | 1,200 | 3,480 | |
| | 4,300 | 11,960 | $2.78 |
| Issues on 19 January | (2,100) | (5,838) | $2.78 |
| | 2,200 | 6,122 | |
| Receipts on 25 January | 1,500 | 4,350 | |
| | 3,700 | 10,472 | **$2.83** |
| Issues on 31 January | (1,800) | (5,094) | **$2.83** |
| | 1,900 | 5,378 | |

**138 A**

| | *Units* | *Unit cost* | *Total* |
|---|---|---|---|
| | | $ | $ |
| Opening inventory | 100 | 3.00 | 300 |
| 3 March receipt | 200 | 3.50 | 700 |
| | 300 | | 1,000 |
| 8 March issue | (250) | 200 at 3.50 | (700) |
| | | 50 at 3.00 | (150) |
| | 50 | 3.00 | 150 |
| 15 March receipt | 300 | 3.20 | 960 |
| 17 March receipt | 200 | 3.30 | 660 |
| | 550 | | 1,770 |
| 21 March issue | (500) | 200 at 3.30 | (660) |
| | | 300 at 3.20 | (960) |
| | 50 | 3.00 | 150 |
| 23 March receipt | 450 | 3.10 | 1,395 |
| | 500 | | 1,545 |
| 27 March issue | (350) | 3.10 | (1,085) |
| Closing balance | 150 | | 460 |

The closing inventory balance represents 50 units at $3 and 100 units at $3.10.

**139 B**

| | *Units* | *Unit cost* | *Total* |
|---|---|---|---|
| | | $ | $ |
| Opening inventory | 100 | 3.00 | 300 |
| 3 March receipt | 200 | 3.50 | 700 |
| | 300 | 3.333 | 1,000 |
| 8 March issue | (250) | 3.333 | (833) |
| | 50 | 3.333 | 167 |
| 15 March receipt | 300 | 3.20 | 960 |
| 17 March receipt | 200 | 3.30 | 660 |
| | 550 | 3.249 | 1,787 |
| 21 March issue | (500) | 3.249 | (1,625) |
| | 50 | 3.249 | 162 |
| 23 March receipt | 450 | 3.10 | 1,395 |
| | 500 | 3.114 | 1,557 |
| 27 March issue | (350) | 3.114 | (1,090) |
| Closing balance | 150 | 3.114 | 467 |

Issues = $833 + $1,625 + $1,090 = $3,548

**140 B**

With FIFO, the issues on 9 September are valued as follows:

| | $ |
|---|---|
| 60 units of the opening inventory brought forward (at $5) | 300 |
| 10 units received on 4 June (at $5.50) | 55 |
| Total value | 355 |

**141 C**

With LIFO, the issues on 9 September are valued as follows:

| | $ |
|---|---|
| 50 units received on 6 June (at $6) | 300 |
| 20 units received on 4 June (at $5.50) | 110 |
| Total value | 410 |

**142 D**

A and C are relevant only to physical inventory movement.

B is a description of the LIFO method.

**143 A**

B and D are incorrect as material costs which are lower, reduce cost.

C is incorrect as lower costs lead to higher profit.

**144 B**

| | *Kg* |
|---|---|
| Required for production (6,000 × 2.5) | 15,000 |
| Required closing inventory (1,800 × 2/3) | 1,200 |
| | 16,200 |
| Expected opening inventory | 1,800 |
| Therefore budgeted purchase quantities | 14,400 |

**145 D**

| | *Units of T* | *Units of X* |
|---|---|---|
| Sales budget | 5,000 | |
| Increase in finished goods inventory | 200 | |
| Production budget | 5,200 | |
| Required for production (5,200 × 3) | | 15,600 |
| Increase in closing inventory | | 400 |
| Therefore budgeted purchase quantities | | 16,000 |

**146 C**

Production budget

| | |
|---|---|
| Sales | 8,000 |
| + closing inventory | 1,500 |
| – opening inventory | 2,000 |
| | 7,500 |

Usage budget = 7,500 units × 1.2 kg per unit = 9,000 kgs

Purchases budget:

| | |
|---|---|
| usage | 9,000 |
| + closing inventory | 2,400 |
| – opening inventory | 1,500 |
| | 9,900 kgs |

# THE SPREADSHEET SYSTEM

**147 C**

By definition.

**148 B**

A spreadsheet program can convert numerical data into the form of a graph, pie chart or bar chart, as required, but it cannot produce a narrative description.

**149 C**

A database contains records and files and is most suitable for storing large volumes of data

**150 B**

All are said to be advantages of spreadsheet software with the exception of (i) security.

A computer-based approach exposes the firm to threats from viruses, hackers and general system failure.

**151 D**

Budgeted production for a period = budgeted sales for the period + closing inventory of finished goods for the period –opening inventory of finished goods for the period.

Here

F3 + 10% of F4 – 10% of F3 = budgeted production for March

**152 B**

Using graphics is usually done using the chart wizard not the format cells option.

**153 A**

B would be done best via a face to face discussion and a spreadsheet would not feature strongly.

C would be best done using a word processing package.

D would be best done using a database.

**154 C**

The correct syntax has an = sign and a colon.

**155 D**

Depending on which number formatting category you select, you will be able to adjust the following characteristics:

| | **Decimal Places** | **Negative number format** | **1000 Separator** | **Currency symbol** |
|---|---|---|---|---|
| **Number** | Yes | Yes | Yes | – |
| **Currency** | Yes | Yes | Auto | Yes |
| **Accounting** | Yes | – | Auto | Yes |
| **Percentage** | Yes | – | – | – |

**156 C**

Depending on which number formatting category you select, you will be able to adjust the following characteristics:

| | **Decimal Places** | **Negative number format** | **1000 Separator** | **Currency symbol** |
|---|---|---|---|---|
| **Number** | Yes | Yes | Yes | – |
| **Currency** | Yes | Yes | Auto | Yes |
| **Accounting** | Yes | – | Auto | Yes |
| **Percentage** | Yes | – | – | – |

**157 C**

In this respect spreadsheets follow the usual rules for the use of brackets

**158 B**

Pie charts will be least effective to show trends but both of the others will work, although you could argue that the line chart is best.

**159 B**

| Error | Description |
|---|---|
| #DIV/0! | This occurs where we have tried to divide by zero or a blank cell. |
| #NAME? | This occurs when we use a name that Excel doesn't recognise. This is common in incorrectly spelled function names |
| #NUM! | This occurs when you place an invalid argument in a function |
| #REF! | This occurs when a formula uses an invalid cell reference |
| #VALUE! | This occurs when we attempt to use an incorrect data type |

**160 C**

| Error | Description |
|---|---|
| #DIV/0! | This occurs where we have tried to divide by zero or a blank cell. |
| #NAME? | This occurs when we use a name that Excel doesn't recognise. This is common in incorrectly spelled function names |
| #NUM! | This occurs when you place an invalid argument in a function |
| #REF! | This occurs when a formula uses an invalid cell reference |
| #VALUE! | This occurs when we attempt to use an incorrect data type |

**161 A**

An entire page is a worksheet (a workbook may have many worksheets) and columns are identified by letters not numbers.

**162 D**

(1) is false – while formula can be copied from one cell to another, the formula in a particular cell will only give the value for that cell. Other cells may then use this answer in their own formulae.

(2) is false – Control+end takes you to the cell furthest into the worksheet that has been active [even if the content has been removed]

**163 A**

Formatting is concerned with appearance and seeks to make the spreadsheet look more interesting and make it reflect the underlying data better. Thus a number format may be better than plain text (hence (4) is wrong). Formatting is not concerned with ordering, so statement (2) is incorrect.

**164 B**

Wrap text increases the height of a row so that all text is visible.

**165 C**

The default print options are portrait, A4 without gridlines.

**166 D**

Line graphs are very useful to demonstrate trends.

**167 D**

Accounting information is usually confidential and should not be given to anyone without the proper authority.

**168 B**

The Ctrl key + P will bring up the Print function, which will then print if you click on OK.

**169 B**

The number will appear as you typed it.

**170 D**

The number will appear with a percentage sign after it. Most Excel spreadsheets will work to two decimal places by default.

**171 A**

Rounding 10.567 will give 11.

**172 B**

The symbol $ makes a cell address absolute.

**173 A**

Total commission = total saes × 5% = (home sales + overseas sales) × 5%

**174 D**

The standard 40 hour week needs to be 'held' to compare with the employees actual hours in cells C10 to C14. Using the $ sign next to B and 2 will do this.

**175 A**

To SORT the price column C, you would need to select the data range A2:C5, right click, data, sort, choose to sort column C.

**176 B**

A component bar chart shows the total sales in any one year. The individual components of each bar should show the sales mix for the three different products.

**177 C**

Given we are looking at a single period, a pie chart would be the most useful for showing the overall split.

**178 D**

Management accounting reports should be understandable by non-financial managers. It is totally misguided to think that all managers should be financially literate, and it is important to make sure that reports to non-financial managers are clear and well presented, and that difficult or unusual issues are explained carefully.

**179 C**

The first two explanations are not related to three dimensional spreadsheets. The final description is not three dimensional as the workbooks are not linked together. Option C is the correct definition.

**180 D**

**181 A**

See Chapter 19, section 7.3 of the text for a full explanation of the round function.

**182 B**

Spreadsheets are commonly used for internal, management accounting information such as variance reports, budgets and forecasts. The annual accounts are more likely to use word processing or publishing software (or even specialist accounting software) as they will involve more words and fewer calculations.

**183 A**

This is the order in which the symbols will be interpreted when entered into a spreadsheet formula.

**184 A**

All selected columns will be hidden. So if three columns are selected, three will be hidden.

**185 B**

It would not be possible to select the hidden row as it is hidden. A user must select the rows above and below the hidden row or rows.

**186 B**

The password to open option would not allow the user to even view the spreadsheet without entering a password. The 'read only recommended' option simply makes a recommendation to the user not to make changes, but the user can choose to make changes if they wish. The password to modify option will prompt the user to enter a password before making changes and is the correct answer.

**187 B**

**188 D**

There must be two parts to the custom format – one for positive numbers and one for negative numbers. So this rules out option A. The two parts must be separated by a semi-colon – this rules out option B. To show negative numbers with brackets the second part of the format must be surrounded by brackets. Therefore, option D is the correct answer.

**189 D**

There must be three parts to the custom format when we want to show zeros as blanks – one for positive numbers, one for negative numbers and one for zeros. So this rules out options A and C. To show zeros as blanks the third part must be blank – this rules out option B. Option D is the correct answer.

**190 C**

The time format must be split by a colon. The other answers will appear as text rather than as a time format (which can then be used in formulae etc.).

**191 B**

The spreadsheet won't recognise the text 'Four' as a number and will remind the user to input a number rather than text.

**192 D**

Option D alludes to a disadvantage of bar charts. If the bar chart is split into components it is more difficult to see the overall total.

**193 C**

Line graphs will identify trends as it will be easy to see upward or downward patterns as well as peaks and troughs for seasonality.

**194 D**

The other graphs/charts rely on some correlation between the variables. A scatter graph is more likely to illustrate a random pattern or non-relationship.

**195 D**

**196 B**

Legend refers to the key and using the legend option allows a user to determine where the key gets displayed on a chart (for example, a user can choose to have it at the side or underneath the chart).

**197 B**

**198 D**

**199 A**

**200 A**

**201 A**

**202 B**

# Section 3

# MOCK EXAM QUESTIONS

**ALL 50 QUESTIONS ARE COMPULSORY AND MUST BE ATTEMPTED**

**1 The following statements relate to financial accounting or to cost and management accounting:**

(i) Financial accounts are historical records.

(ii) Cost accounting is part of financial accounting and establishes costs incurred by an organisation.

(iii) Management accounting is used to aid planning, control and decision making.

**Which of the statements are correct?**

A (i) and (ii) only

B (i) and (iii) only

C (ii) and (iii) only

D (i), (ii) and (iii)

**2 Which of the following is *not* necessarily a quality of good management information?**

A Timeliness

B Relevance

C Understandability

D Prudence

**3 Which of the following statements concerning data and information is true?**

A Information and data are two words used to describe the same thing.

B Information consists of raw facts and figures that have yet to be processed.

C Data consists of information that has been processed in a predefined way.

D Information consists of data that has been processed in a predefined way.

**4** Payments to suppliers are entered into an integrated computerised accounting system.

**Which of the following does *not* happen when these payments are entered into the computerised system?**

A The supplier's individual account is updated in the purchase ledger/payables ledger.

B The payables control account in the nominal ledger (main ledger) is debited.

C The bank account in the nominal ledger is credited.

D The receivables control account in the nominal ledger is credited.

**5 Integrated accounts application packages have a number of advantages. Which of the following is *not* one of them?**

A User-friendly, as the functions will be similar in each module

B Tailored to suit the requirements of the business

C Compatibility between the modules

D Efficiency, as there is no need to quit one application to access another

**6 In a large organisation, which of the following individuals is most likely to authorise the payment of a purchase invoice for goods bought from a supplier?**

A manager with appropriate authority in the:

A accounts department

B buying department

C department that requisitioned the goods

D stores department

**7 What is the main purpose of books of prime entry?**

A Assist the preparation of financial statements

B Assist the monthly bank reconciliation

C Provide a check on the double-entry bookkeeping

D Prevent unnecessary detail in the ledgers

**8 Noel is considering introducing a number of control systems into his business. However, he is uncertain about what this would accomplish. Which of the following is NOT a purpose of organisational control systems?**

A Safeguarding of company assets

B Prevention of errors

C Increased profitability

D Increased efficiency

**9 In an interlocking accounting system what would be the correct double entry for the issue of direct materials from a warehouse?**

| | | |
|---|---|---|
| A | Dr Raw material inventory | Cr Work in progress |
| B | Dr Raw material inventory | Cr Production overhead |
| C | Dr Work in progress | Cr Raw material inventory |
| D | Dr Production overhead | Cr Raw material inventory |

**10** Management information is used at different levels of the organisation

(i) Information used by strategic management tends to be summarised.

(ii) Information used by strategic management tends to be forward looking.

(iii) information used by operational management tends to contain estimates.

(iv) information used by operational management tends to be required frequently.

**Which of the above statements are true?**

A (i), (ii) and (iv) only

B (i), (iii) and (iv) only

C (ii) and (iii) only

D (iii) and (iv) only

**11 What document may be used to authorise the issue of items from the stores department to a user department?**

A Purchase order

B Delivery note

C Requisition note

D Goods received note

**12** The current inventory position for inventory item 35528 is as follows:

| | *Units* |
|---|---|
| Held in inventory | 14,500 |
| On order from supplier | 36,300 |
| Requisitioned | 16,700 |

**What is the free inventory for this item?**

A 0

B 5,100 units

C 34,100 units

D 38,500 units

**13** The following documents are used within a cost accounting system:

(i) invoice from supplier

(ii) purchase order

(iii) purchase requisition

(iv) stores requisition

**Which TWO of the documents are matched with the goods received note in the buying process?**

A (i) and (ii)

B (i) and (iv)

C (ii) and (iii)

D (iii) and (iv)

**14 Which of the following items of cost cannot be treated as a sales and distribution overhead expense within a manufacturing business?**

A Cost of after-sales service to customers

B Telephone charges

C Cost of building insurance

D Warehouse rental for storage of raw materials

**15** An engineering business has a department with a work force of eight engineers and one supervisor. The department carries out small engineering jobs for business customers.

**Which of the following costs would be treated as a direct expense of a particular job for a customer?**

A Supervision costs

B Cost of delivery of equipment to the customer

C Depreciation of engineering equipment

D Cost of engineer's time on the job

**16 Which of the following is an example of external information?**

A Idle time reports

B Sales price lists

C Health and safety regulations

D Accident at work reports

**17 Which ONE of the following would be classified as direct labour?**

A Personnel manager in a company servicing cars

B Cleaner in a cleaning company

C General manager in a DIY shop

D Maintenance manager in a company producing cameras

**18** **Which of the following may be used to support claims for overtime payments for salaried staff?**

A Employee record cards

B Job cards

C Payslips

D Timesheets

**19** In accounting systems, data is usually organised using codes.

**Which one of the following statements about codes is *incorrect*?**

A Using codes helps to improve the speed and accuracy of data processing

B Using codes allows more data validation checks to be carried out

C A hierarchical code structure makes it easier to find items on a code list, since similar items are grouped

D Codes in accounting reduce the need for accountants to understand the principles of accounting

**20** Gregs Ltd operates from four main sites. In analysing its costs (overheads) it uses a nine digit coding system. A sample from the coding manual shows:

| *Site* | | *Expenditure type* | | *Function* | |
|---|---|---|---|---|---|
| Wokingham | 100 | Rent | 410 | Purchasing | 600 |
| Windsor | 200 | Power | 420 | Finance | 610 |
| Winchester | 300 | Heat and light | 430 | Production | 620 |
| Warwick | 400 | Travel costs | 440 | Sales | 630 |

The order of coding is: site/expense/function

**An invoice for the Windsor site for travel costs for sales teams would be coded as:**

A 200/410/600

B 200/420/610

C 200/430/620

D 200/440/630

**21** The performance of an investment centre is measured by residual income. In a particular period, the investment centre had fixed assets of $200,000 and net current assets of $40,000. Its annual profits were as follows:

| | $ | $ |
|---|---|---|
| Sales price | | 217,000 |
| Direct costs of the division | 175,000 | |
| Apportioned head office costs | 15,000 | |
| Total divisional costs | | 190,000 |
| Profit | | 27,000 |

The notional interest on capital is 8%.

**What was the residual income for the centre for the year?**

A $7,800

B $11,000

C $22,800

D $26,000

**22** **Which of the following measures of performance is unsuitable for a profit centre?**

A Sales income per employee

B Profit as a percentage of sales revenue

C Return on capital employed

D Cost per machine hour operated

**23** **Which of the following statements is incorrect?**

A There may be several investment centres within a single organisation

B There may be several cost centres within an investment centre

C There may be several cost centres within a profit centre

D There may be several profit centres within a cost centre

**24** **In a system of absorption costing, why are the absorption rates for fixed overheads usually determined in advance, as part of the budget, instead of retrospectively at the end of the budget period?**

A It is simpler to decide overhead rates in advance than retrospectively.

B It is not possible to calculate actual overhead costs retrospectively.

C So that fixed overheads can be charged to output before the end of the accounting period.

D Predetermined overheads are more accurate than overhead costs calculated retrospectively.

**25** **The annual costs of supervision in a department are estimated to be $40,000 if hours worked in the department are less than 32,000 each year, $65,000 if hours worked are between 32,000 and 50,000 and $80,000 if hours worked are over 50,000 in the year. These costs are an example of:**

A a semi-fixed cost

B a fixed cost

C a stepped cost

D a variable cost

**26** You are presented with the following information about sales and costs for a business that makes and sells a range of products:

| | $ |
|---|---|
| Sales revenue | 320,000 |
| Direct labour | 100,000 |
| Direct material | 75,000 |
| Production overhead | 78,000 |
| Other overhead costs | 50,000 |

The business uses absorption costing. There were no opening or closing inventories of the product.

**What profit would be reported for the period, using absorption costing?**

A $15,000

B $17,000

C $20,000

D $23,000

**27** **Which of the following statements IS true when applied to fixed costs:**

A Overhead costs are always fixed costs

B As production levels increase, fixed cost per unit decreases

C Fixed costs are always irrelevant in a decision making situation

D as the level of activity changes, fixed costs will also change

**28** **Which of the following cost classifications is most useful for forecasting?**

A Direct v indirect

B Production v non-production

C Fixed v variable

D Controllable v non-controllable

**29** Hannah works as a trainee accountant for a large accountancy firm. She is salaried and each month completes a time sheet indicating how much time she has spent working on which clients. In March Hannah's time was fully utilized on client work but she didn't do any overtime.

**From her firm's perspective, how should Hannah's salary costs for March be classified?**

| | | |
|---|---|---|
| A | Fixed | Direct |
| B | Fixed | Indirect |
| C | Variable | Direct |
| D | Variable | Indirect |

**30** A company achieves bulk buying discounts on quantities of raw material above a certain level. These discounts are only available for the units above the specified level and not on all the units purchased.

**Which of the following graphs of total purchase cost against units best illustrates the above situation?**

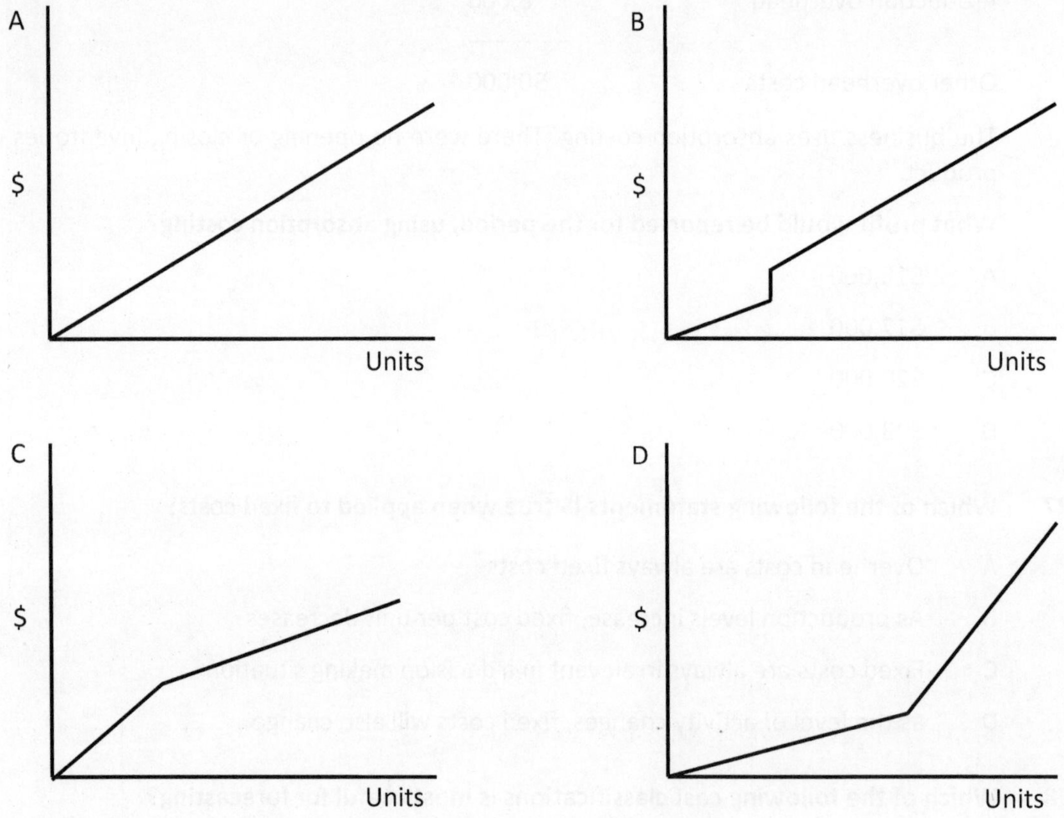

**31** A direct labour employee receives a wage of $8 per hour for a 38-hour week, with time + 25% for overtime. During a particular week, the employee worked for 42 hours. Due to an equipment breakdown and the late delivery of urgent materials from a supplier, the employee had to record six hours of idle time for the week.

**What amount will be charged as a direct labour cost for the employee's work in the week?**

A $288

B $296

C $304

D $336

**32** A manufactured product requires two units of raw materials, each costing $5. The following budget decisions have been made for the next budget period.

| | |
|---|---|
| | *Product units* |
| Sales volume | 9,000 |
| | *Materials units* |
| Opening inventory of raw materials | 3,500 |
| Closing inventory of raw materials | 2,800 |

**What is the raw materials purchase requirement for the period?**

A $76,500

B $83,500

C $86,500

D $93,500

**33** The following information is available for a small business with three departments, A, B and C that all operate in the same building.

| Department | *A* | *B* | *C* |
|---|---|---|---|
| Floor area (square metres) | 1,500 | 2,000 | 1,500 |
| Number of employees | 10 | 6 | 4 |
| Assets | $40,000 | $40,000 | $80,000 |
| Labour hours per month | 1,200 | 1,000 | 800 |

Employees are provided with free lunchtime meals, and the cost of this small 'canteen' service is $1,800 per month.

**If the businesses uses an absorption costing system, what would be the most appropriate charge to department A each month for the cost of the canteen service?**

A $540

B $900

C $450

D $720

**34** The following data relates to a company's payroll for the month just ended:

| | $ |
|---|---|
| Paid to employees | 67,000 |
| Employees' National Insurance contributions | 21,000 |
| Employer's National Insurance contributions | 13,200 |
| Income tax | 36,300 |
| Employer's contribution to employees' pension fund | 15,000 |

**What is the total labour cost for the month?**

A $152,500

B $139,300

C $137,500

D $124,300

**35** A product uses 6 kilograms of raw material and takes two direct labour hours to make. Raw materials cost $2.50 per kilogram and direct labour is paid $4 per hour. Variable production overheads are 25% of labour costs. The budgeted fixed production costs for the year were $120,000 and budgeted direct labour hours were 20,000 hours. Fixed overheads are recovered on a direct labour hour basis.

**The full production cost per unit of product is:**

A $25

B $31

C $35

D $37

**36** **Which of the following would operate a job costing system?**

A Shipbuilder

B Oil refinery

C Steel producer

D Kitchen fitter

**37** Completed output from a manufacturing process in a period totalled 5,640 units. There was no work-in-progress at the beginning of the period but 780 units, 60% complete, remained in the process at the end of the period.

**What are the equivalent units of the closing work-in-progress?**

A 312

B 468

C 780

D 6,108

**38** A manufacturing process had no work-in-progress at the beginning of a period. 20,000 units of raw material, costing $8.20 per unit, were input to the process in the period. 18,600 completed units were transferred out. Conversion costs were $7.65 per completed unit and $6.12 per incomplete unit.

**What was the value of the closing work-in-progress?**

A $8,568

B $20,048

C $22,190

D $30,788

**39** A company values stocks using the weighted average value after each purchase. The following materials receipts and issues were made last month:

| *Date* | *Receipts* | | | *Issues* |
|---|---|---|---|---|
| | *Units* | *$/unit* | *Valuation* | *Units* |
| Brought forward | 100 | $5.00 | $500 | |
| 4th | 150 | $5.50 | $825 | |
| 16th | | | | 100 |
| 20th | 100 | $6.00 | $600 | |
| 21st | | | | 75 |

**What is the value of the closing stock using this weighted average method?**

A $1,012.50

B $976.50

C $962.50

D $925.00

**40 A firm has a high level of stock turnover and uses the FIFO (first in first out) issue pricing system. In a period of rising purchase prices, the closing stock valuation is:**

A close to current purchase prices

B based on the prices of the first items received

C much lower than current purchase prices

D the average of all goods purchased in the period

**41 Which of the following symbols are used in spreadsheet software?**

(i) /

(ii) *

(iii) ^

(iv) ×

A (ii) and (iii)

B (i), (ii) and (iii)

C (ii), (iii) and (iv)

D All of them

**42 Which of the following are disadvantages of spreadsheets?**

(i) Inability to efficiently identify data errors

(ii) Finite number of records

(iii) Most data managers are familiar with them

(iv) Lack of detailed sorting and querying abilities

A (i) and (iv)

B (i), (iii) and (iv)

C (i), (ii) and (iv)

D All of them

**43 Which of the following are advantages of spreadsheet software over manual approaches?**

(i) Security

(ii) Speed

(iii) Accuracy

(iv) Legibility

A All of them

B (ii), (iii) and (iv)

C (ii) and (iv)

D (i) and (iv)

**44 For which of the following tasks would a computer spreadsheet be most useful?**

A Cost coding structure

B Product listing

C Staff appraisal

D Variance analysis

**45 A business wants to organise its operational data into a computer system for the entire organisation that will allow multiple-user access to files. Which of the following types of general-purpose application package would be most suitable for this purpose?**

A Word processing

B Spreadsheet

C Integrated accounts

D Database

**46** The following spreadsheet shows an extract from a company's sales figures.

| | A | B | C | D | E |
|---|---|---|---|---|---|
| 1 | **Sales** | | 2011 | 2012 | 2013 |
| 2 | **Region** | | | | |
| 3 | N | | 10,000 | 12,000 | 11,500 |
| 4 | S | | 7,000 | 6,200 | 8,200 |
| 5 | E | | 3,000 | 10,000 | 12,000 |
| 6 | W | | 1,500 | 5,750 | 5,600 |

The management accountant wishes to produce a chart to demonstrate the trends over time between the different regions and is considering the following charts:

(i) Stacked (compound) bar chart

(ii) Line charts

(iii) Pie charts

**Which of the charts would be suitable?**

A (i) only

B (i) and (ii)

C (ii) only

D (i), (ii) and (iii)

**47** Examine the following spreadsheet extract:

| | A | B | C | D |
|---|---|---|---|---|
| 1 | **Sales Month** | **Product X** | **Product Y** | **Total** |
| 2 | Jan | 10,000 | 50,000 | 60,000 |
| 3 | Feb | 14,000 | 6,000 | 20,000 |
| 4 | Mar | 12,000 | TBC | |

**The formula in cell D2 is: =B2+C2. If this formula was copied to cell D4, which error message would appear?**

A #DIV/0!

B #VALUE!

C #REF!

D #NAME?

**48 To unhide a hidden row, a user must first select**

A The entire worksheet

B The entire workbook

C The row that is hidden

D The rows above and below the hidden row

**49** Examine the following spreadsheet extract for a budget calculation:

| | A | B | C |
|---|---|---|---|
| 1 | **Budget for May** | | **$000** |
| 2 | Sales | | 120 |
| 3 | Cost of sales | | (50) |
| 4 | Gross profit | | 70 |
| 5 | Selling and distribution costs | | (30) |
| 6 | Operating profit | | 40 |

**Which formula in cell C6 will give the correct figure for the operating profit?**

A =SUM(C2:C5)

B =C4-C5

C =C2-C3-C5

D =SUM(C4:C5)

**50 Which of the following are reasons for formatting data in a spreadsheet?**

(1) To make text (i.e. labels) more visually interesting

(2) To get data into the correct order for analysis

(3) To make numbers more descriptive of what they represent

(4) To make the data appear as plain text

A (1) and (3) only

B (2) and (3) only

C (2) and (4) only

D (1), (2) and (3)

Section 4

# ANSWERS TO MOCK EXAM QUESTIONS

**1 B**

Cost accounting is not part of financial accounting.

**2 D**

Prudence is a desirable quality in financial accounting information, for reporting to shareholders. However, it is not necessarily a quality in management information. Management might wish to be prudent when making their judgements and decisions, but they do not need prudence in the information they receive.

**3 D**

By definition

**4 D**

This question is not testing your knowledge of debits and credits. It is checking that you understand the basic workings of an accounts system. When a payment is made to a supplier, a single entry into the integrated computer system will update the supplier's individual account in the payables/creditors/purchase ledger, and it will update the bank account and the payables control account in the nominal ledger. The receivables control account is unaffected by payments to suppliers.

**5 B**

With an integrated accounts system, the system consists of several applications or modules, such as nominal ledger, sales ledger, purchase ledger, inventory control system, payroll, management accounting, and so on. Each module is compatible with the others, and functions are similar in each module. They are efficient, because a user does not have to quit one module to enter another (which would be necessary if the accounts system consisted of different non-integrated applications).

However, when an integrated system is purchased 'off-the-shelf' (i.e. when it is an 'applications package') the user must take it as it comes, and the system is not tailored exactly to the user's requirements.

**6 B**

The accounts department should be instructed to make the payment, but should not authorise the payment itself. The authorisation for a payment should come from the department that can check that the purchase invoice details agree with the purchase order details and the goods received note details. The purchase order will not be seen by the stores department, nor by the department requisitioning the goods.

**7 D**

The main purpose of books of prime entry is to allow the main double entry into the nominal ledger to comprise totals – for example posting the total sales for the month to the sales account rather than showing every individual invoice.

**8 C**

Control systems may indirectly improve profitability through increased efficiency, etc., but it is not one of their primary purposes.

**9 C**

The credit entry must recognise that the materials have been taken out of inventory, so answers A and B are incorrect. Given the materials are "direct", then the debit entry must be to WIP (C) rather than overheads (D).

**10 A**

(iii) is incorrect as operational level information is usually accurate.

**11 C**

A materials requisition note is a document requesting materials from stores. It should be signed by a person with authority to make the requisition.

**12 C**

| | *Units* |
|---|---|
| Held in inventory | 14,500 |
| On order from supplier | 36,300 |
| | 50,800 |
| Requisitioned | 16,700 |
| Free inventory | 34,100 |

**13 A**

An invoice is matched to a goods received note and a purchase order before payment is made.

**14 D**

Sales and distribution overhead costs should include telephone charges for telephones used by the sales and distribution department and the costs of after-sales service. The sales and distribution department should also receive an apportioned share of building insurance costs for the building it occupies.

In a manufacturing business, rental costs for the raw materials warehouse are a production overhead cost.

**15 B**

A direct cost is a cost that is directly attributable. Here, the direct costs of the job are the costs that are directly attributable to that job. Supervision costs and depreciation of equipment are general overhead costs for the department, and so would be treated as overheads. The costs of delivery and wages costs are both direct costs, but the wages cost is a direct labour cost. The delivery charge would be a direct expense.

**16 C**

External information is information that comes from outside the organisation, and is not generated from within the organisation. It includes rules and regulations from external bodies, government statistics, tax rates, information from customers or suppliers, and so on. Price lists for the organisation's own products, idle time records and accident records are all internal information.

**17 B**

Cleaner in a cleaning company.

The cleaner's wages can be identified with a specific cost unit therefore this is a direct cost. The wages paid to the other three people cannot be identified with specific cost units. Therefore they would be indirect costs.

**18 D**

**19 D**

Statements A, B and C are all correct. When codes are used, more data validation checks (such as existence checks, range checks and check digit checks) are possible. As a result, data processing should be more accurate. Codes are shorter than a description of the items they represent, so using codes speeds up processing too. A hierarchical code is also useful for learning and accessing code items. Using codes does not take away the need to understand the work that is being done or the items that are being processed, so statement D is incorrect.

**20 D**

**21 A**

| | $ |
|---|---|
| Profit | 27,000 |
| Notional interest (8% × $240,000) | 19,200 |
| Residual income | 7,800 |

**22 C**

Performance measures for a profit centre should include measures of profit, such as gross profit margin and net profit margin (profit to sales ratio). They might also include measures of performance relating to sales income (e.g. sales per employee) and performance relating to cost (e.g. cost per machine hour).

An unsuitable measure of performance for a profit centre is one that relates profits to capital employed (ROCE). ROCE could be a suitable performance measure for an investment centre.

**23 D**

Cost centre, profit centres and investment centres are often organised in a hierarchy, with several cost centres in a profit centre, several profit centres in an investment centre and several investment centres in an organisation. There will not be several profit centres (manager responsible for revenues and costs) in a cost centre (manager responsible for costs only).

**24 C**

If the budget period is one year, it would be inconvenient to wait up to one year to calculate the actual overhead costs of production retrospectively. Using a predetermined overhead rate gets round this problem, although as a consequence, there will be some under-absorbed or over-absorbed overheads.

**25 C**

This is a stepped cost. A stepped cost is a cost that is fixed within a certain range of activity levels, but then changes if the activity level rises above or falls below that range to a new 'fixed' level. In this example, supervision costs will rise as activity increases as more supervisory staff have to be employed.

**26 B**

| | $ | $ |
|---|---|---|
| Sales revenue | | 320,000 |
| Direct labour | 100,000 | |
| Direct material | 75,000 | |
| Production overhead | 78,000 | |
| | | 253,000 |
| | | 67,000 |
| Other overhead costs | | 50,000 |
| Profit | | 17,000 |

**27 B**

**28 C**

When forecasting it is key to understand cost behaviour

**29 A**

Hannah's salary does not depend on whether or not she works on client work or doing general admin, hence her salary cost is fixed.

The fact that Hannah completes a timesheet allows her firm to apportion her salary costs to clients, hence her salary costs are direct.

**30 C**

Raw materials are a variable cost so the graph will begin at the origin and increase at a gradient equal to the cost per unit. The cost per unit falls at a certain point so the gradient will become less and the graph will be flatter. Option D shows a situation where the cost per unit becomes greater above a certain volume.

**31 A**

| | *Hours* |
|---|---|
| Total hours worked | 42 |
| Idle time | 6 |
| Hours actively worked | 36 |
| Basic rate per hour | $8 |
| Direct labour cost | $288 |

The overtime premium for the four hours of overtime, and the cost of the six hours of idle time, will be treated as an indirect labour cost.

**32 C**

| | |
|---|---|
| Sales volume (units) | 9,000 |
| Raw materials units per product | 2 |
| | *Units of material* |
| Materials usage budget | 18,000 |
| Add closing inventory required | 2,800 |
| Less opening inventory available | (3,500) |
| Materials purchases (units) | 17,300 |
| Cost per unit | $5 |
| Materials purchase budget in $ | $86,500 |

**33 B**

Presumably, each employee receives the same benefits from the service, therefore the most suitable basis for apportioning the cost should be the number of employees in each department. Department A should therefore be charged with $1,800 × (10/20) = $900.

**34 A**

| | $ |
|---|---|
| Paid to employees | 67,000 |
| Employees' National Insurance contributions | 21,000 |
| Income tax | 36,300 |
| Gross pay | 124,300 |
| Employer's National Insurance contributions | 13,200 |
| Employer's contribution to employees' pension fund | 15,000 |
| Total labour cost | 152,500 |

Gross earnings are the total earnings of employees. The employer must pay in addition the employer's National Insurance contributions, and if there is a pension scheme for employees, the employer's contributions into the scheme are also an additional labour cost.

**35 D**

The fixed production overhead absorption rate is $120,000/20,000 hours = $6 per direct labour hour.

| | $ |
|---|---|
| Direct materials (6 kg × $2.50) | 15 |
| Direct labour (2 hours × $4) | 8 |
| Variable production overhead (25% of 2 hours × $4) | 2 |
| Fixed production overhead (2 hours × $6) | 12 |
| Full production cost per unit | 37 |

**36 D**

Kitchen fitting consists of short jobs for customers, with each job being different. A shipbuilder will operate a contract costing system, and an oil refinery and a steel producer are likely to have process costing systems.

**37 B**

Closing work-in-progress is 780 × 0.6 = 468.

Total equivalent units for the period are 5,640 + 468 = 6,108.

**38 B**

1,400 × $14.32 = $20,048

There are no losses in the process so there are 20,000 – 18,600 = 1,400 units of work-in-process. These are valued at $8.20 + $6.12 = $14.32.

**39 B**

**Receipts and issues**

| *Units* | *Price per unit* | *Cost* |
|---|---|---|
| | $ | $ |
| 100 | 5.00 | 500.0 |
| 150 | 5.50 | 825.0 |
| 250 | 5.30 | 1,325.0 |
| (100) | 5.30 | (530.0) |
| 150 | | 795.0 |
| 100 | 6.00 | 600.0 |
| 250 | 5.58 | 1,395.0 |
| (75) | 5.58 | (418.5) |
| 175 | 5.58 | **976.5** |

**40 A**

FIFO means that the value of closing stock reflects the most recent prices paid.

**41 B**

× is not used for multiplication, the * symbol is.

**42 C**

(iii) is an advantage.

**43 B**

All are said to be advantages of spreadsheet software with the exception of (i) security. A computer-based approach exposes the firm to threats from viruses, hackers and general system failure.

**44 D**

**45 D**

A database can be used to organise operational data that allows different users to access the same files for their data processing requirements. An integrated accounts package is insufficient for handling all the operational data of an organisation.

**46 B**

Pie charts will be least effective to show trends but both of the others will work, although you could argue that the line chart is best.

**47 B**

The spreadsheet won't recognise the text 'TBC' as a number and will remind the user to input a number rather than text.

**48 D**

It would not be possible to select the hidden row as it is hidden. A user must select the rows above and below the hidden row or rows.

**49 D**

The formula in A is no use as it includes subtotals (e.g. cell C4) in the summation, resulting in figures effectively being double counted. B and C are no use as they deduct costs that have been entered as negative numbers (so need to be added).

**50 A**

Formatting is concerned with appearance and seeks to make the spreadsheet look more interesting and make it reflect the underlying data better. Thus a number format may be better than plain text (hence (4) is wrong). Formatting is not concerned with ordering, so statement (2) is incorrect.

FOUNDATIONS IN ACCOUNTANCY

# Management Information

Specimen Exam applicable from June 2014

**Time allowed:** 2 hours

ALL 50 questions are compulsory and MUST be attempted.

**Do NOT open this paper until instructed by the supervisor.**

**This question paper must not be removed from the examination hall.**

**The Association of Chartered Certified Accountants**

# Paper MA1

ACCA

**ALL 50 questions are compulsory and MUST be attempted**

Please use the space provided on the inside cover of the Candidate Answer Booklet to indicate your chosen answer to each multiple choice question.
Each question is worth 2 marks.

1 **Which of the following may be a cost centre?**

- **A** One of the hotels owned by a leisure company
- **B** The accountancy department in a business
- **C** The direct material cost of a product
- **D** The total depreciation expense of a business

2 All of a company's workers are paid the same hourly rate.

The following spreadsheet is to be used to calculate wages earned by different workers each week. A formula is entered in cell B4 and then a fill command is used to copy this formula into cells C4 to G4.

| | A | B | C | D | E | F | G |
|---|---|---|---|---|---|---|---|
| 1 | Wage rate per hour ($) | 12 | | | | | |
| 2 | Worker | P | Q | R | S | T | U |
| 3 | Hours worked | 40 | 28 | 38 | 39 | 40 | 27 |
| 4 | Wages earned ($) | | | | | | |
| 5 | | | | | | | |
| 6 | | | | | | | |

**Which of the following formulae should be entered into cell B4 prior to using the fill command to make sure that the correct formulae is used for cells C4 to G4?**

- **A** =B1*B3
- **B** =$B$1*B3
- **C** =B1*$B$3
- **D** =$B$1*$B*$3

3 There was no work-in-progress in a manufacturing process at the start of a period. 18,000 units of a product commenced processing in the period during which completed output was 16,100 units. The work-in-progress was 75% complete for conversion costs which were $4·60 per equivalent unit. There were no losses or gains in the process

**What amount was included in the closing work-in-progress for conversion costs?**

- **A** $6,555
- **B** $8,740
- **C** $11,653
- **D** $18,515

4 **Which of the following statements is true?**

- **A** Information consists of raw facts that have not been processed
- **B** Data consists of information
- **C** Data consists of processed information
- **D** Information consists of data which has been processed in a predefined way

5 **For which of the following tasks would a computer spreadsheet be most useful?**

**A** Expense coding structure
**B** Product listing
**C** Staff appraisal
**D** Cost analysis

6 Receipts and issues of a raw material for a period were:

| | units | $ per unit | cumulative total $ |
|---|---|---|---|
| Day 1 balance | 160 | 3·70 | 592 |
| Day 3 receipt | 230 | 3·60 | 1,420 |
| Day 5 issue | 110 | | |
| Day 8 issue | 150 | | |

**Using the LIFO inventory pricing method, what is the total cost of the issue on Day 8?**

**A** $540
**B** $543
**C** $545
**D** $555

7 Product X is manufactured by Y Co. Direct materials cost $6·10 and prime costs total $9·60 per unit of product. Production overheads are absorbed at a rate of $13·40 per machine hour. Two units of Product X are manufactured per machine hour.

**Using absorption costing, what is the total production cost per unit of Product X?**

**A** $16·30
**B** $22·40
**C** $23·00
**D** $29·10

8 **Which of the following is a major advantage of the use of computer spreadsheets in management accounting?**

**A** Formulas are consistent in that they usually appear as numbers
**B** They can be printed and hard copies filed
**C** They can be used to record the cost coding structure
**D** What-if analysis can be carried out easily and quickly

9 Product X requires 1·8 kg of a raw material per finished unit. The material has a weight loss of 10% in preparation for manufacture. Inventory of the material is currently 420 kg but needs to be increased to 500 kg. 2,000 units of Product X are to be manufactured.

**How many kg of the raw material need to be purchased to satisfy the above requirements?**

**A** 3,880
**B** 3,920
**C** 4,040
**D** 4,080

**10** At the end of a period the percentage completion of the work-in-progress in a continuous manufacturing process was over estimated.

**What effect would correction of the error have on the cost per equivalent unit and the total cost of output completed in the period?**

| | Unit cost | Cost of output |
|---|---|---|
| **A** | Decrease | Decrease |
| **B** | Decrease | Increase |
| **C** | Increase | Decrease |
| **D** | Increase | Increase |

**11 What is the purpose of prime entry records?**

**A** Assist the preparation of a trial balance
**B** Prevent unnecessary detail in the ledgers
**C** Provide a check on the double-entry bookkeeping
**D** Provide a list of outstanding payments

**12** The following scatter graph plots nine observed sets of data from a factory.

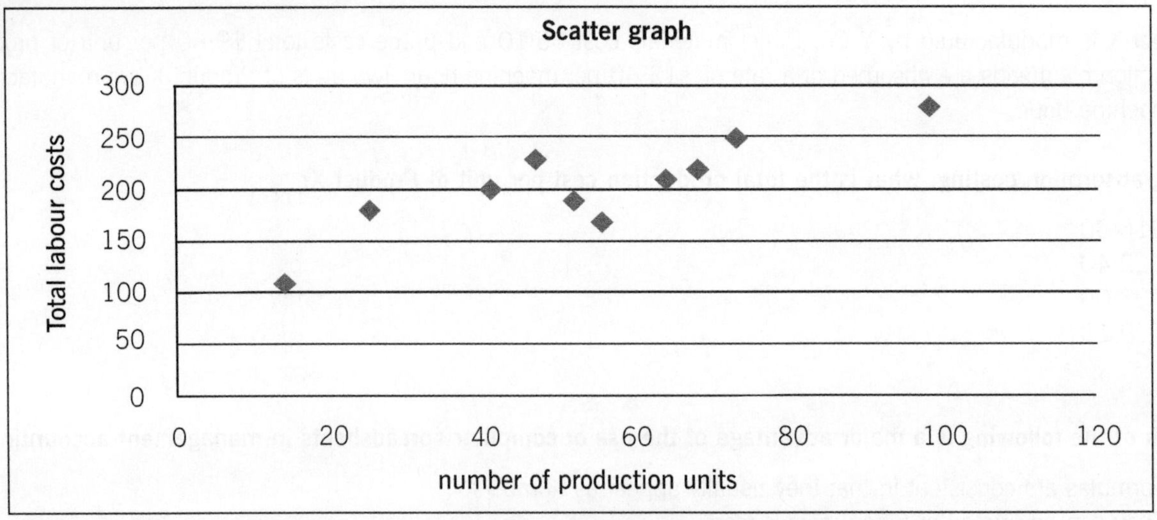


**Which term would BEST describe the behaviour of total labour cost?**

**A** Fixed cost
**B** Stepped – fixed cost
**C** Semi-variable cost
**D** Variable cost

**13** A production operative is paid $11·00 per hour for a basic 35-hour week. Overtime is paid at 40% over the basic rate. The operative worked for 38 hours in week 9. Income tax deducted was $76·40 and benefit contribution payments were:

| | |
|---|---|
| Employer | $40 |
| Employee | 10% of gross pay |

**What was the net pay of the operative in week 9?**

**A** $271·68
**B** $311·68
**C** $316·30
**D** $319·29

**14** No losses or gains occur in a manufacturing process. There was no work-in-progress at the start of a period during which 9,600 litres of a raw material were input to the process. 8,700 litres of finished product were output from the process in the period. The stage of completion of the work-in-progress was:

| | |
|---|---|
| Materials | 100% |
| Conversion costs | 60% |

**What were the equivalent units of production in the period?**

| | Materials | Conversion costs |
|---|---|---|
| **A** | 8,700 | 8,700 |
| **B** | 8,700 | 9,060 |
| **C** | 9,600 | 9,240 |
| **D** | 9,600 | 9,600 |

**15 Using marginal costing, what is the basis for valuing inventory of finished goods in a manufacturing business?**

**A** Direct + indirect production costs
**B** Prime costs + total variable costs
**C** Prime costs + variable production overheads
**D** Production costs + variable non-production costs

**16 What is a time sheet used for?**

**A** To calculate pay only
**B** To charge cost centres for work done only
**C** To record attendance time
**D** To calculate pay and to charge cost centres for work done

**17 Which of the following documents will MOST help a sales manager to monitor the effectiveness of a sales team?**

**A** A monthly report comparing sales targets with actual results
**B** The sales department's organisational chart
**C** A monthly report analysing the reasons for customer complaints
**D** The completion of appraisal interview forms

**18** The following financial figures relate to Jolly for a year:

| | 20X2 |
|---|---|
| | $ |
| Sales | 50,000 |
| Cost of sales | (10,000) |
| Gross profit | 40,000 |
| Expenses | (15,000) |
| Net profit | 25,000 |
| Capital employed | 100,000 |

**What is the asset turnover ratio for 20X2?**

**A** 0·8 times
**B** 0·4 times
**C** 2 times
**D** 0·5 times

**19** The following spreadsheet shows a company's statement of profit or loss for the coming period.

| | A | B | C | D | E |
|---|---|---|---|---|---|
| 1 | Statement of Profit or Loss | | | | |
| 2 | Period 2 | | | | |
| 3 | | Division A | Division B | DivisionC | Total |
| 4 | Sales Revenue | 5,000 | 6,000 | 8,000 | 19,000 |
| 5 | Variable costs | 1,500 | 1,800 | 2,400 | 5,700 |
| 6 | Contribution | 3,500 | 4,200 | 5,600 | 13,300 |
| 7 | Fixed cost | 2,000 | 3,000 | 4,000 | 9,000 |
| 8 | Profit | 1,500 | 1,200 | 1,600 | 4,300 |
| 9 | | | | | |
| 10 | | | | | |

**Which of the following formulae is correct for calculating the value of cell E8?**

**A** =Sum(B8:D8)
**B** Sum(B8:D8)
**C** =Sum (E4:E7)
**D** Sum (E4:E7)

**20 Which activity is LEAST likely to be the responsibility of the accounting function of a large organisation?**

**A** Calculation of wages
**B** Control of trade receivables
**C** Dispatch of customer orders
**D** Payment of trade payables

**21** A spreadsheet includes the following pie chart to analyse a company's total manufacturing cost for a period. The company's production overhead in the period was $124,700.

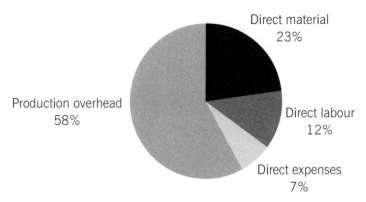

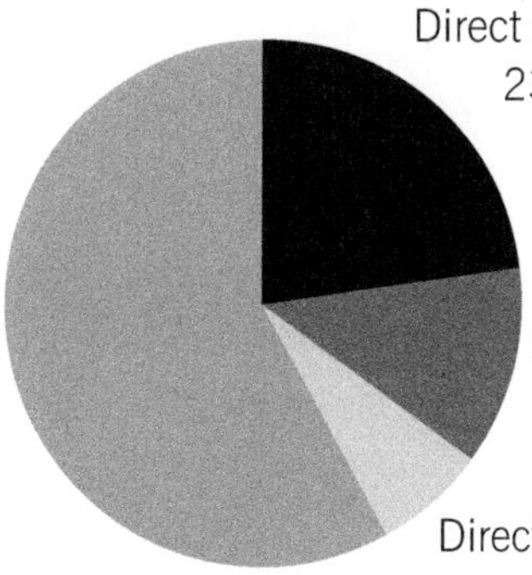


**What are the total direct costs?**

**A** $43,645
**B** $52,374
**C** $53,750
**D** $90,300

**22** A Business has the following results:

| | $ |
|---|---|
| Sales | 100,000 |
| Cost of sales | (20,000) |
| Gross profit | 80,000 |
| Expenses | (30,000) |
| Net profit | 50,000 |

**What is the net profit margin for the Business?**

**A** 50%
**B** 80%
**C** 62·5%
**D** 200%

**23 What is the effect of using brackets in a spreadsheet formula?**

**A** Divisions and multiplications are calculated before additions and subtractions
**B** Additions and subtractions are calculated before divisions and multiplications
**C** The contents of the brackets are calculated first
**D** The contents of the brackets are calculated last

**24** A differential piecework payment scheme applies to direct workers in a production cost centre, subject to a guaranteed minimum wage of $50 per day. The differential rates for output each day are:

| | |
|---|---|
| up to 100 units | $0·50 per unit |
| excess over 100 units | $0·60 per unit |

A worker produced the following over a three-day period:

| | |
|---|---|
| Day 1 | 100 units |
| Day 2 | 90 units |
| Day 3 | 110 units |

**What is the worker's total wages for the three days?**

**A** $151
**B** $156
**C** $161
**D** $166

**25 What is the purpose of an organisation chart?**

**A** To demonstrate formal relationships and communication flows
**B** To demonstrate the filing and coding systems used
**C** To map where each department and function is located
**D** To set out production schedules for a period

**26** A manufacturer absorbs production overheads into the cost of jobs as a percentage of actual direct labour cost. Two jobs were worked on during a period:

| | Job 1 ($) | Job 2 ($) |
|---|---|---|
| Opening work-in-progress | 5,269 | – |
| Direct materials in the period | 10,726 | 4,652 |
| Direct labour in the period | 4,360 | 2,940 |

Production overheads of $9,855 were incurred in the period. Job 2 was completed in the period.

**What is the value of work in progress at the end of the period?**

**A** $20,972
**B** $24,941
**C** $26,241
**D** $20,355

**27** A Management Accountant wishes to present the following spreadsheet information in a chart.

| | Direct cost | Production overheads | Non-production overheads | Total cost |
|---|---|---|---|---|
| Factory 1 | 80 | 30 | 30 | 140 |
| Factory 2 | 200 | 50 | 40 | 290 |
| Factory 3 | 70 | 20 | 40 | 130 |

She is considering using the following charts:

(i) Scatter diagram
(ii) Line chart
(iii) Stacked (compound) bar chart

**Which chart(s) would be most appropriate?**

**A** (i) and (iii)
**B** (ii)
**C** (iii)
**D** (i) and (ii) only

**28** The following indirect costs were incurred in a factory in a period:

| | |
|---|---|
| Rental of premises | \$80,000 |
| Utilities | \$25,000 |

There are two cost centres, A and B, in the factory which between them occupy the 20,000 square metres (sq m) of floor space (cost centre A, 8,000 sq m; cost centre B, 12,000 sq m).

**What is the total indirect cost apportionment to cost centre B in the period if floor space is used as the basis of apportionment?**

**A** \$42,000
**B** \$52,500
**C** \$63,000
**D** \$105,000

**29** You have been asked to write a report outlining the qualities of good information.

**Which of the following would you NOT include in the report?**

**A** The information should be complete
**B** The information should be communicated via an appropriate channel
**C** The information should be understandable
**D** The information should be communicated to everyone in the organisation

**30** **In an interlocking accounting system what would be the entry for the issue of indirect material?**

| | | |
|---|---|---|
| **A** | Dr Raw material inventory | Cr Work in progress |
| **B** | Dr Raw material inventory | Cr Production overhead |
| **C** | Dr Work in progress | Cr Raw material inventory |
| **D** | Dr Production overhead | Cr Raw material inventory |

**31** A coding system uses a combination of letters and numbers to classify costs. The first two digits of each code represent the cost centre, the third and fourth digits represent the type of expense and the fifth and sixth digits represent the detail of the expense.

Relevant codes for a particular expense are:

| | **code** |
|---|---|
| Selling expense | 24 |
| Northern division | ND |
| Commission | SC |

**What is the correct code for the above expense?**

**A** SC24ND
**B** NDSC24
**C** ND24SC
**D** 24SCND

**32 Which of the following are reasons for formatting data in a spreadsheet?**

(1) To get data into the correct order for analysis
(2) To make labels visually interesting
(3) To make numbers more descriptive of what they represent
(4) To make the data appear as plain text

**A** 1 and 3 only
**B** 2 and 3 only
**C** 2 and 4 only
**D** 1, 2 and 3

**33** Direct operatives in a factory are paid on a time rate basis for a 35-hour week.

**If productivity can be improved what will happen to direct labour costs per unit of output?**

**A** Decrease
**B** Increase
**C** No change
**D** Not possible to determine from the information provided

**34 Which of the following statements concerning spreadsheet cells are correct?**

(1) A formula in a particular cell may calculate numbers for several cells
(2) Clicking on a particular cell, and then entering a number or text, will enter data into that single cell
(3) Each cell can contain a number, a label or a formula
(4) Press Shift and Enter to select the cell below in the same column

**A** 1, 2 and 4
**B** 1, 3 and 4
**C** 2 and 3 only
**D** 3 and 4 only

**35 Which of the following statements concerning the recording and analysis of sales are TRUE?**

(1) The sales figure that should be taken from an invoice is net of both trade discount and sales tax
(2) Sales may be analysed in a number of different ways for management accounting purposes

**A** Both 1 and 2
**B** 1 only
**C** 2 only
**D** Neither 1 nor 2

**36 Which of the following are features of useful management information?**

(1) Communicated to the right person
(2) Provided whatever the cost
(3) Sufficiently accurate for its cost

**A** (1) only
**B** (1) and (3) only
**C** (2) and (3) only
**D** (1), (2) and (3)

**37 Which item would most likely be treated as an indirect cost by a furniture manufacturer?**

**A** Fabric to cover the seat of a chair
**B** Metal used for the legs of a chair
**C** Staples to fit the fabric to the seat of a chair
**D** Wood used to make the frame of a chair

**38 Which of the following is TRUE about the effect of different methods of pricing raw materials from inventory in a period of consistently rising prices?**

(1) Production costs will be higher using FIFO rather than LIFO
(2) Closing inventory values will be lower using periodic weighted average rather than cumulative weighted average

**A** 1 only
**B** 2 only
**C** Both statements
**D** Neither statement

**39 In an inventory control system, what is normally meant by free inventory?**

**A** Inventory which is available for new orders from customers
**B** Inventory which is available for promotional offers
**C** Inventory which is in transit from supplier to warehouse
**D** Inventory which is in transit from warehouse to customer

**40 What is the charging of an overhead cost directly to a cost centre known as?**

**A** Overhead absorption
**B** Overhead allocation
**C** Overhead apportionment
**D** Overhead assignment

**41 Which of the following states the responsibility of the manager of a profit centre?**

A Responsibility for revenues but not costs
B Responsibility for costs but not revenues
C Responsibility for revenues and costs
D Responsibility for revenues, costs and investment

**42 Which of the following defines cost classification?**

A The grouping of costs according to their common characteristics
B The allotment of items of cost to cost centres
C The sum of all costs incurred
D The use by several companies of the same costing methods

**43 Which of the following are correct descriptions applied to computer spreadsheets?**

(1) An entire page of rows and columns is called a workbook
(2) Each row is identified by a letter
(3) Data is organised in rows and columns
(4) The intersection of each row and column defines a cell

A 1 and 2 only
B 2 and 4 only
C 3 and 4 only
D 1, 2, 3 and 4

**44** Production labour costs incurred during a period included the following items:

| | |
|---|---|
| (1) Salary of factory manager | $2,400 |
| (2) Training of direct workers | $1,660 |
| (3) Normal idle time | $840 |
| (4) Overtime premiums of direct workers | $2,760 |
| (5) Overtime hours of direct workers at basic rate | $9,200 |

**What total amount would usually be charged to production overhead for the above items?**

A $4,060
B $4,900
C $7,660
D $16,860

**45 Which of the following are features of an efficient and effective coding system?**

(1) Each item should have a unique code
(2) Each code should contain a combination of letters and numbers
(3) Each code should completely disguise the item being coded
(4) Codes should not be uniform in length and structure

A 1 only
B 1 and 2 only
C 1, 3 and 4 only
D 2, 3 and 4 only

**46 Which of the following is normally treated as a direct labour cost?**

**A** Controllable idle time
**B** Uncontrollable idle time
**C** Overtime premium due to a temporary backlog in production
**D** Overtime premium at the specific request of a customer

**47** 25,000 units of a company's single product are produced in a period during which 28,000 units are sold. Opening inventory was 7,000 units. Unit costs of the product are:

| | $ per unit |
|---|---|
| Direct costs | 16·20 |
| Fixed production overhead | 7·60 |
| Fixed non-production overhead | 2·90 |

**What is the difference in profit between absorption and marginal costing?**

**A** $22,800
**B** $30,400
**C** $31,500
**D** $42,000

**48** A sales representative earns a basic salary of $10,000 per annum, a guaranteed end-of-year bonus of $5,000 and 5% commission on the value of sales.

**What cost classification is appropriate for the sales representative's salary?**

**A** Direct cost
**B** Product cost
**C** Semi-fixed cost
**D** Prime cost

**49** Consider the following tasks:

(1) Setting selling prices for products and services
(2) Analysing departmental expenditure for control purposes
(3) Calculating the quantity of raw materials in store
(4) Calculating wages for employees working on special shifts

**Which tasks are likely to be carried out by a trainee accountant?**

**A** 1 and 2 only
**B** 1, 3 and 4 only
**C** 2, 3 and 4 only
**D** 1, 2, 3 and 4

**50** TRS CONSULTANTS
31 Oxford Avenue
Milton Mewbury
Lincolnshire

Invoice number: 9911

Date: 25 February 20X1

Customer:
Jacqueline Smith
ACCA
2 Central Quay
Glasgow
G3 8BW

Item:
Accountancy training $1,500·00

**In the integrated computerised accounts of TRS Consultants, which of the following is correct?**

**A** The bank account will be credited
**B** The sales account will be debited
**C** Trade payables control account will be debited
**D** Trade receivables control account will be debited

**(100 marks)**

**End of Question Paper**

# Answers

1 **B**

2 **B**

3 **A**
(18,000 – 16,100)*·75*$4·60 = 6,555

4 **D**

5 **D**

6 **B**
((230 – 110)*3·60) + (3·7*(150 – (230 – 110))) = $543

7 **A**
Overhead costs per unit:
13·4 ÷ 2 = 6·7
Total production cost per unit:
6·7 + 9·60 = 16·30

8 **D**

9 **D**
Material required per finished unit with a 10% loss:
1·8 ÷ ·90 = 2
Total material required for manufacture:
2*2,000 = 4,000
Total materials to buy:
4,000 – 420 + 500 = 4,080

10 **D**

11 **B**

12 **C**

13 **B**
Basic pay (35*11) = 385
Overtime pay (11*1·40)*(38 – 35) = 46·2
Gross pay (385 + 46·20) = 431·20
Benefit contribution (431·2*·1) = 43·12
Net pay ($431·20 – $76·40 – $43·12) = $311·68

14 **C**
Output 8,700
WIP (9,600 – 8,700) = 900
Equivalent units:

| | **Material costs** | **Conversion costs** |
|---|---|---|
| Finished goods | 8,700 | 8700 |
| WIP | 900 (900*100%) | 540 (900* 60%) |
| Total | 9,600 | 9,240 |

15 **C**

16 **D**

17 **A**

18 **D**
Sales/capital employed
50,000/100,000
0·5 times

19 **A**

20 **C**

21 **D**
Total direct costs percentage: (23 + 12 + 7) = 42%
Total direct costs: (124,700/58%) *42% = $90,300

2 **A**
(Net profit/ sales)*100
(50,000/100,000)*100
50%

**C**

**24 B**

Day 1 pay (100*0·5) = $50
Day 2 pay (90*0·5) = 40 but get minimum = $50
+ day 3 pay (100*0·5) + (10*0·6) = $56
Total = $156

**25 A**

**26 C**

Overhead production cost for Job 1
(4,360/(4,360 + 2,940))*9,855 = $5,886
Total costs (5,269 + 10,726 + 4,360 + 5,886) = $26,241

**27 C**

**28 C**

Percentage occupancy for centre B
12,000/(8,000 + 12,000) = 60%
Overheads apportioned to B
(80,000 + 25,000)*60%
$63,000

**29 D**

**30 D**

**31 C**

**32 B**

**33 A**

**34 C**

**35 A**

**36 B**

**37 C**

**38 B**

**39 A**

**40 B**

**41 C**

**42 A**

**43 C**

**44 C**

(2,400 + 1,660 + 840 + 2,760) = 7,660

**45 A**

**46 D**

**47 A**

**48 C**

**49 C**

**50 D**